will value the way she has woven biblical and theological insights together with her own warmhearted message. Dana Robert is herself a friend in the church's need."

— Fleming Rutledge,
author of *The Crucifixion*

"When we follow Jesus, we discover along the way that God blesses us with the gift of friendship. These relationships, in turn, make a life of faithfulness, hope, and joy possible. Dana Robert is one of our most distinguished missiologists, and in *Faithful Friendships,* her reflections are deeply rooted in the gospels, in richly varied stories of Christian mission, and in our own need for the diverse gifts of the people God places along our journeys."

— Ken Carter, Bishop, Florida Conference,
The United Methodist Church

"Poignant portrayals of sacrificial and joyous, subversive and life-giving friendships. Deep friendships that untie knots of binding nationalism, racial, ethnic and cultural difference and become seeds for societal healing and reconciliation. Robert's offering is a provocative invitation to all who yearn for God's goodness in the world."

— Ruth Padilla DeBorst,
World Vision International

"Refusing to be torn apart by wars, revolutions, and systemic injustice and oppression, the individuals in *Faithful Friendships* manifest their faith and humanity in noble acts of friendship that defies the boundaries of race, nationality, class, religion, and culture. An inspiring read."

— Xi Lian, Duke Divinity School

Faithful Friendships

Embracing Diversity in Christian Community

Dana L. Robert

WILLIAM B. EERDMANS PUBLISHING COMPANY
GRAND RAPIDS, MICHIGAN

Wm. B. Eerdmans Publishing Co.
4035 Park East Court SE, Grand Rapids, Michigan 49546
www.eerdmans.com

25 24 23 22 21 20 19   1 2 3 4 5 6 7

ISBN 978-0-8028-2571-1

Library of Congress Cataloging-in-Publication Data

A catalog record for this book is available from the Library of Congress.

CONTENTS

CONTENTS

FOREWORD

Early in her book, Dana Robert writes that "friendship is intimate and ordinary. It can also be revolutionary: it points to God's kingdom" (6). That insight captures a central element of what makes this book wonderful—descriptions of, and reflections on, the surprising capacity of faithful friendships to cross major cultural and social boundaries while providing a vision of the beauty and richness of God's kingdom. Stories of courage, fidelity, and generosity illustrate how friendships can cross generations, genders, and social and cultural differences. The book is an invitation and challenge to enter into the generally overlooked world of unusual friendships.

Dana's use of stories to tell the larger story of cross-cultural friendship is part of what makes this book distinctive. The author is both a historian and a missiologist, and her book demonstrates the good fruit that grows when a historian's love for retrieving wisdom from the past is combined with a missiologist's passion for the present. Dana draws particular insights about friendship from missional settings across history—a resource largely overlooked as a site for wisdom about cross-cultural relationships. The particularity of friendship is replicated in the particularity of her stories.

While recognizing that friendship cannot "do" everything, she nevertheless makes significant claims for its importance, not least of which are her observations that "friendship makes us human," and friendships "form individuals, create neighborhoods and churches, and knit together the fabric of society" (1). She also suggests that "for Christians today, the cultivation of risk-taking friendships is an ethical and spiritual imperative" (3). Her accounts also show that friendship is an extraordinary joy and privilege for those who share in it—it changes all involved and adds immeasurably to their lives and understandings of discipleship.

In virtue ethics, friendship has long been recognized as an important practice, but few ethicists have attended to the rich potential and dynamic complexity present in friendships that involve major cultural or social differences. Dana Robert's careful attention to this provides a window into the power of cross-cultural friendship to help form us in virtue—especially the virtues of wisdom, fidelity, hospitality, and justice. While recognizing that friendship has limitations in addressing structural injustices or political challenges, she demonstrates how friendship can shape people into individuals able to see such challenges and injustices with fuller clarity and more personal commitment.

God's love is the starting point for Christian friendship, Dana explains, and Jesus's life, in community with his disciples, provides us with a powerful model for cross-cultural friendships. Citing arguments that friendship "is the most important single force behind people becoming Christian" (15) she reminds readers that when Christians think about mission we tend to turn to the Great Commission and Great Commandment passages in Matthew, but we often miss the important "relational implications of following Jesus—namely, love for specific persons who are the unique and beloved children of God" (14). When followers are rooted in the love, power, and model of Jesus, we are able to form friendships with joy, humility, and grace, even across difficult borders and high boundaries. Her emphasis on the importance of friendship in Christian mission—while not making it a tool of evangelism or using it instrumentally—is one of the book's most important contributions to mission practice and moral reflection.

Her stories also warn us that cross-cultural friendships are often costly. A choice for friendship can involve leaving behind loyalties to family, tribe, or nation. "Exile from one's friends, and exile for the sake of one's friends" can leave faithful Christians without an earthly home. There are, as she notes, no "cheap" friendships in true cross-cultural relationships (99). In the midst of ethnic or social divisions or national warfare, friendships often require and elicit courage, as friends can be caught in the middle, rejected by both sides or viewed as traitors or collaborators. However, as she notes, when friends move forward together "they cocreate a new narrative of grace" (113).

Dana is sensitive to critiques of mission as handmaiden to "racist expansionism" and sees her book as offering a "counter narrative in which Christians have done their best, through specific cross-cultural friendships," to reject imperialism and prejudice (188). While recognizing that "friendship does not eliminate racism, ethnocentrism, and other injustices" and "is not a substitute for political action or structural change," she argues that friendship does change the people involved (185). She identifies the risks of power differences, colonialism, and racism in forming cross-cultural friendships, but she also describes friends who "saw their cross-cultural, transnational friendship as a deliberate Christian witness against colonialism and racism, and a statement of hope in building the kingdom of God" (65). Such friendships bring joy, growth, and hope, while they also demonstrate an alternate reality.

Books about friendship are sometimes viewed as lightweight or tame, but this book is bold in its recognition of the value of risky, truth-filled friendships, especially today when we have so many opportunities to use friendships to reinforce our own prejudices and assumptions. Like any significant human practice, friendship can seem safe and predictable, unless it is at odds with the larger culture, or when it challenges our deepest assumptions, privilege, and sin.

Friendship is about individual lives woven together by fidelity, love, and a shared story that grows over time. Dana's book is like that—we are drawn into stories of friendships that are shaped by and express the light of the kingdom. She does not back away from difficulty or claim that friendship "works." She does provide insightful, true, and complicated stories. Not all of them have happy endings, but each is a testimony to the significance and power of friendship.

I am delighted to be able to encourage readers of this book to dive deep into its wisdom and grace. Dana quotes Matteo Ricci, who wrote that "if friendship were to disappear from this world, then the world would, without a doubt, come to an end" (31). This book reminds us that Christian friendship "carries in its core the joy of resurrection" (166). In an age fraught with cultural tension, international disagreement, and frequent displays of ill will, faithful friendships are not too little, too late. Instead, they are surely among our best hopes for reconciliation, healing, and Christian witness.

CHRISTINE D. POHL
January 2019

ACKNOWLEDGMENTS

This book has been a long time coming, and I owe many people thanks for encouraging me along the way and for sparking ideas that eventually made their way into the book.[1] In 2015, I gave the Parchman Endowed Lecture Series at Baylor University's George W. Truett Theological Seminary in Waco, Texas. My ideas further developed into the Sprunt Lectures at Union Presbyterian Seminary in Richmond, Virginia, in 2017. This book represents the expansion and revision of the Sprunt Lectures. And so especially to Mike Stroope of Truett Seminary, and Stanley Skreslet and his students at Union Presbyterian Seminary, I say thanks for your warm hospitality and helpful suggestions.

I deeply appreciate the various conversations I have had on the subject of Christian friendship. I am thankful for patience and encouragement from my husband, Inus Daneel, as well as permission to share some of his story. I appreciate the supportive comments and suggestions from Wilbert Shenk, Grant Wacker, Chris Rice, Elizabeth Parsons, Bonnie

Sue Lewis, Roger Olson, Peter Weaver, and Courtney Goto. Special thanks go to Glen Messer and Daryl Ireland for their careful reading of the manuscript. Greer Cordner, Kelly Fassett, Kathryn Heidelberger, and Allison Kach provided timely encouragement when we discussed the manuscript in a seminar at the Boston University School of Theology. Soojin Chung and Tyler Lenocker critiqued the manuscript, and also worked on the notes and saved me from petty errors. Alex Mayfield prepared the helpful index. David Bratt of Eerdmans has given valuable feedback at crucial points in the writing process.

Research for this manuscript would not have been possible without support from the Historical Society's Religion and Innovation in Human Affairs project from 2012 to 2014. Although the major publication for that project is still in process, early ideas for this book were developed in tandem and tried out in the lectures listed above. I thus owe Donald Yerxa a huge debt of gratitude for giving me the space to reflect on this subject. I drafted the book when I was on sabbatical as a Henry Luce III Fellow in Theology in 2016–17. Dean Mary Elizabeth Moore of the Boston University School of Theology allowed me time off for this project, and I am grateful for her steady encouragement. To Stephen Graham, the Association of Theological Schools, and the Luce Foundation, I give hearty thanks. Part of my sabbatical was spent at the Leibniz Institute of European History (IEG) in Mainz, Germany, where I wrote a couple of chapters. The warm and supportive atmosphere of the IEG helped me keep my equilibrium after my husband had an accident and endured five surgeries during four weeks of hospitalization in Mainz. Director Irene Dingel, Barbara Müller, librarian

Silvia Hoffmann, and fellow researcher Michael Snape were particularly helpful. To Judith Becker especially, I owe many thanks.

I dedicate this book to friends near and far, and to my sons, Sam and John.

INTRODUCTION

It is a miracle, but it happens.

—Hugh Black, *Friendship*

Friendship is both ordinary and revolutionary. Long the subject of poets and sages, friendship makes us human. It involves giving and receiving, and mutual trust. Friendships form individuals, create neighborhoods and churches, and knit together the fabric of society. If we cannot imagine others as potential friends, and therefore as equal to ourselves, then we cannot survive on a planet that gets smaller all the time.

But modern society is experiencing a friendship crisis of epic proportions. For example, lack of friends has worsened the problem of loneliness. Studies show that an estimated 20 percent of Americans are lonely.[1] Millions are lonely old people, stuck in the homes in which they raised their kids, living without friends or family nearby. The problem of loneliness in the United Kingdom has gotten so bad that the government has hired a "minister for loneliness." Loneliness creates severe health problems and affects employment productivity. In Japan, elderly people dying alone has become a new normal.

Technology is another factor that limits face-to-face interaction. Articles on the influence of social media show that while interconnection and digitization are more common than ever before, they are a poor substitute for direct human contact. People spend so much time checking the newsfeed on their cell phones that they have stopped saying hello or chatting in casual conversations. Isolation in one's own bubble becomes the norm. "We live in an accelerating contradiction: the more connected we become, the lonelier we are. We were promised a global village; instead we inhabit the drab cul-de-sacs and endless freeways of a vast suburb of information."[2]

On a community level, the crisis of friendship worsens when it comes to cross-cultural and cross-ethnic relationships. Neighborhoods are full of people of diverse origins, religions, and lifestyles, and interracial relationships are more possible than ever before. But anxiety about crossing boundaries seems to be increasing. In theological seminaries across the United States, I see students raising questions about whether it is even possible to be friends with persons of other races or political persuasions. Systemic injustices, racism, arguments over migration, and internet trolling are creating situations in which enemies seem to outnumber friends.

On the global level, resentment of the ethnic or racial "other" can cause withdrawal rather than embrace of new opportunities to make friends with people from other countries. Theologian Hugh Black wrote in his treatise *Friendship* over a century ago that "to act on the worldly policy, to treat a friend as if he might become an enemy, is of course to be friendless."[3] And friendlessness leads to personal, social, and political collapse. The poet John Donne named the deeper issues at stake when he wrote how the disconnection of even one person was both a personal loss and a diminishment of the totality of humanity: "No man is an island, entire of itself. . . . Any man's death diminishes me, because I am involved in mankind, and therefore never send to know for whom the bell tolls; it tolls for thee."[4]

In the face of enduring human divisions, not to mention the fragmentation of modern society, this book insists that Christians have the responsibility to make friends across divisions that separate us from one another. For Christians today, the cultivation of risk-taking friendships is an ethical and spiritual imperative. When followers of Jesus Christ retreat from the personal responsibility to create diverse and loving communities, they betray the gospel of Jesus Christ.

Down through the ages, the followers of Jesus have dared to believe that faithful friendship is not only possible but necessary. This book is about Christians who practiced respect, forgiveness, compassion, humility, sharing, giving, and receiving in mutuality. Of course they were imperfect and limited. Yet their friendship with God inspired them to befriend others. Thus it is important to tell their stories. Although many of the stories I recount took place in missional situations, the insights they provide can inspire friendships, whether in one's own church, neighborhood, or abroad. Walking together, faithful friends embody the connections that reduce loneliness, challenge injustice, and strengthen the fabric of shared community. Embracing diversity through friendship celebrates what it means to be children of God.

Jesus told his followers that the kingdom of God is like a small mustard seed that eventually grows into such a big tree that birds can build nests in its shadow (Mark 4:30–32).[5] I show in this book that faithful friendships across human boundaries can be the mustard seed in Jesus's parable. Although specific friendships do not solve the enduring human problems of division, violence, sin, greed, and oppression, they nevertheless cultivate life "for the healing of the nations" (Rev. 22:2).

Friendship forms Christian identity. The model for friendship is the life of Jesus and his disciples. Jesus had friends. Those friends shared his friendship with others. Expanding networks of friendships traveled across time and place. Obviously not all friendships are between Christians. Yet, embracing diverse friendships—both within the church and outside it—is essential to practicing Christian hope. To make friends witnesses to Christian community in all its promise and vulnerability. In their love for others, including people unlike themselves, Christians show what it means to follow Jesus Christ together. The practice of friendship, therefore, creates Christian community.

In 2011, I flew to Chicago for the hundredth anniversary of the Catholic Foreign Mission Society of America, more popularly known as the Maryknoll Fathers and Brothers.[6] The Maryknollers, a name that encompasses three distinct organizations with a shared history, are the oldest Catholic foreign-missions religious community in North America. They sent pioneer missionaries to China and Latin America. They worked among the poor, mobilized women, and even stared down military dictators—activities for which their community paid the price of martyrdom. As the Protestant representative at the conference, I felt even more excited to be there when, right before my speech, the organizers announced that a special speaker had arrived.

A few feet in front of me stood a small, elderly Peruvian priest. Famous as the father of liberation theology, Father Gustavo Gutiérrez had suffered during the 1960s and 1970s, an era of persecution against the church by Latin American dictators. As a young priest in Peru, Father Gustavo worked closely with the Maryknoll Fathers and Sisters, who lived among the poor—walking beside them in friendship, studying the Bible with them, and working to improve their lives. Father Gustavo had played a big role in helping convince the assembled Catholic bishops to endorse the idea that God has a "preferential option for the poor" at their 1968 assembly in Medellín, Colombia.[7]

As he spoke into the microphone, Father Gustavo asked, "What is the meaning of the preferential option for the poor?" He paused, then answered his own question: "The meaning of the preferential option for the poor is to be friends with the poor. I am here because the Maryknollers are my friends."

When Father Gustavo proclaimed that the North American Sisters and priests were his friends, he was talking about the kinds of friendship narrated in this book. He did not mean mere self-fulfillment, though of course friendship is intensely personal. He did not mean friendship in a short-term, "here today, gone tomorrow" sense. He was not referring to the number of "likes" he received on social media. He did not mean friendship as "random acts of kindness." He did not mean friendship with people exactly like himself. Rather, by *friendship*, Father Gustavo meant shared discipleship—faithful obedience to the God of love, walking together in equality with and respect for specific persons whom God loves, and caring for the world God loves.

This book shows that faithful friendships are difficult but not impossible. Each one seems like a miracle. Friendship is intimate and ordinary. It can also be revolutionary: it points to God's kingdom.

About This Book

I have written this book from the perspective of a historian who is also a lay theologian of Christian mission. Readers will quickly realize that this is not a book on the philosophy of friendship, a survey of contemporary practices of friendship as mission, or a systematic study of diversity. Here I use historical narrative rather like a laboratory for current practices.[8] What has cross-cultural friendship looked like, at a personal level, in the building of human community, and in shaping Christian communities? What do these examples teach us about the challenges and promises of friendship? Telling stories of faithful friendships suggests a narrative approach to theology that reflects lay and women's traditions, including those of Wesleyan and Pentecostal perspectives, in which a core question is, "What has God done in your life and in the lives of others?" Theologizing through sharing life stories assumes that followers of Jesus Christ are living simultaneously in the world and in the biblical narrative, and do not willingly separate the two.[9]

The book opens with two introductory chapters. The first chapter suggests biblical foundations for faithful friendship in the life of Jesus, as depicted in the Gospel of John. The second chapter introduces Christian discourses and practices of friendship through key examples in modern history. The heart of the book, chapters 3 through 6, explores biographies of exemplary Christians who, over the past century, have embraced cross-cultural friendship as a central aspect of their Christian identities. In this section, I have identified four interrelated spiritual practices that are common to boundary-crossing friendships: those of remaining or being present, of exile, of testimony, and finally of friendship as joy or celebration. All four of these dimensions characterize cross-cultural Christian friendships to a greater or lesser degree. I have resisted giving a hard-and-fast definition of friendship. Each of the people profiled in these chapters named him- or herself as a friend to others mentioned in the chapter. The meaning of friendship is thus defined in the practice of believing in it, doing it, and calling it by name. The concluding chapter of the book contains my reflections on the meaning and challenges of cross-cultural friendship for US Christians today. In the face of isolation and human fragmentation, faithful friendships are a Christian practice, a deliberate, disciplined set of commitments in which the ideals of compassion, equality, peace, and justice merge with concrete human relationships.[10] Together these commitments build living communities. Stories of friendship show that sacrificial love in Christ bypasses the binaries of the old 1970s argument over evangelism versus social justice. Mutual love among people of different races, cultures,[11] nations, generations, and social classes (or even different political opinions!) testifies to the God of love.

I hope this book contributes to reflection on what it means to be a Christian in the interconnected, multicultural world of today. We all know, deep down, that relationships are the stuff of life. Without a focus on sacrificial relationships across time and place, the inner dynamics of Christian community remain hidden in the shadows. Despite the challenges, I am absolutely certain that diverse, cross-cultural friendship is both a key to the meaning of Christian community and an example of the mustard seed about which Jesus spoke. Like Gustavo Gutiérrez, I believe that love across differences is real.

Friendship has limitations. It does not solve all the world's problems. It does not cure cancer or HIV/AIDS. It does not eliminate structural injustice. It does not involve perfect people who practice perfect mutuality. Friendship is not an adequate social policy or political ideology. Yet, as theologian Emmanuel Katongole wrote in 1994 in the aftermath of genocidal violence in Rwanda, "We engage in mission to establish friendships that lead to the formation of a new people in the world."[12] Faithful friendships dare to witness to Jesus Christ and his final words of encouragement to his disciples: "No one has greater love than this, to lay down one's life for one's friends. You are my friends if you do what I command you" (John 15:13–14).

CHAPTER 1

Founding Community

Jesus and His Friends

No one has greater love than this, to lay down
one's life for one's friends. You are my friends if
you do what I command you.

—John 15:13–14

To be a Christian is to know Jesus. Knowing Jesus is a relationship so intimate that he carries his followers' burdens.
He brings them joy. He walks beside them. In short, Jesus
befriends those who follow him. And friendship with Jesus
builds Christian community across cultural, social, and ethnic
divisions.

In 1909, a young Japanese Protestant, Toyohiko Kagawa,
moved into Shinkawa slum in Kobe. His new neighborhood
was marked by filth, grinding poverty, infectious diseases,
violent crime, prostitution, and a high infant mortality rate.
Kagawa's holistic work among the poor included evangelism,
feeding programs, and health care. His experience in the
slums taught him that charity to the poor was not enough,

so he organized various social movements to improve society. During his early ministry, thousands of Japanese were drawn to Christianity through his potent combination of stirring sermons and practical social work. In October 1921, with fourteen companions, he founded the Friends of Jesus as an intentional Christian community focused on care for the poor. The group prayed together, pooled their income, went on retreats, and supported a settlement house as a base for social outreach.[1] By its ten-year anniversary, the community numbered approximately 1,300 people, both men and women. For Kagawa, to be a friend of Jesus meant living in sacrificial love for the poor and needy, just as Jesus did.

Melkite Archbishop Elias Chacour recalls that as a child growing up in Palestine in the 1940s, he would walk the hills that Jesus walked and speak to Jesus as his "special friend." For his beloved mother too, "peace came not from habit or ritual words, but from talking to a dearly respected Friend—One who cared for us."[2] The Chacour family's intimate relationship with Jesus, whom young Elias thought of as his "champion," gave the family strength when they were displaced from their land. It carried him through theological training in Israel, and into his calling as a priest working among the Palestinian people. Chacour's childhood friend Jesus guided him in peacebuilding between Israelis and Palestinians.

In 1993, the Reverend Dr. Margaret Moshoeshoe Montjane was an Anglican chaplain at the huge Baragwanath Hospital in the South African township of Soweto. She was a former student of mine, and I was scheduled to go visit her. Then on April 10, a right-wing nationalist murdered the head of the South African Communist Party, Chris Hani, in his driveway. Immediately riots broke out throughout the country, especially in Soweto. South Africa was a powder keg, and Nelson Mandela could barely keep the lid on. Angry young men surged into Baragwanath Hospital with their injured comrades. Margaret used all her authority to avert rioting in the hospital, ordering the rioters to sit down and treat the hospital with respect. When we spoke on the phone before my scheduled visit, I asked her how she was managing. She answered, "Without Jesus, I couldn't get through the day."

Jesus is my friend, and I am his. As seen in the examples above, this assurance is shared by believers around the world. To be a friend is to know oneself in relation to another. Friends are committed to common values and interests. Definitions of friendship are also shaped by cultural norms and therefore can differ across cultures, age groups, social classes, and genders. The meaning of friendship changes over time. To speak of Jesus as friend, therefore, may not mean the same thing to all people. But to claim Jesus as friend means to share a sense of powerful belonging, and to claim a relationship with other friends of Jesus as well.

In most cultures, the idea of friendship is a powerful statement of relational identity. In Batak culture in Indonesia, for example, it is said that the loss of a friend is worse than the loss of one's mother. Traditional Russian culture assumes it is better to have many friends than much money. In Confucian tradition, friendship is one of the basic relationships that undergirds society. For American Christians, being friends with Jesus tends to be personal. When asked to put the word "Jesus" and "friend" together, Americans think of familiar hymns like "What a Friend We Have in Jesus," "Jesus Is All the World to Me," and "I've Found a Friend, O Such a Friend!" Comforting songs about Jesus being my friend have been staples of Protestant piety over the past two centuries. Jesus is *my* friend. He carries *my* burdens.

But a cross-cultural perspective on Jesus as friend says a lot about the meaning of community. For friendship always goes both ways. It requires mutuality. It involves give and take. If Jesus is our friend, then doesn't it follow that we are his? Since Jesus is holding hands with the world, so to speak, then intimacy with Jesus extends far beyond personal needs. To befriend Jesus means carrying in fellowship the responsibilities of friendship that he carried. Kagawa, Chacour, and Montjane knew this when they worked for peace and justice despite overwhelming challenges.

Friendship with Jesus, and with others through him, is a core value of Christian identity and practice. Friendship requires both being a friend and acting like one—both being and doing. Without friendship, the family of faith would not exist. In the context of worldwide community, being friends with Jesus is hard work. For when followers of Jesus walk beside him, he leads them in directions they would rather not go, into neighborhoods they would rather avoid, and to meet other friends of his they might not normally know. As the Scriptures and history show, to be a friend of Jesus means loving others just as he does.

Friendship with Jesus in the Gospel of John

The Gospel of John is foundational for the ideas and practices of faithful friendships.[3] First is to state the obvious but neglected fact: Jesus had friends, and he connected God's love to those friendships. From a Christian perspective, God's unselfish love is the starting point for friendship. Willard Swartley notes that the Gospel of John and the epistles 1–3 John contain over 10 percent of usages of words for *love* in the entire Bible.[4] The Gospel of John is the relational gospel, the gospel of love—of agape and *phileo*. It is filled with rich and unique passages about the importance of friendship in Jesus's life and ministry. In chapter 13, for example, Jesus washes the feet of his disciples. Through this loving action he demonstrates the importance of servant leadership. The Gospel of John reflects the perspective of the "beloved disciple," the one Jesus loved. In it, Jesus spends his final night before his arrest praying for his friends. They, in turn, spend the rest of their lives sharing his message with the rest of the world.

The original model for Christian friendship is thus the life and mission of Jesus himself, in community with his disciples. The Gospel of John reports that as Jesus faced death, he counseled his followers to love one another: "No one has greater love than this, to lay down one's life for one's friends. You are my friends if you do what I command you" (John 15:13–14). Sharing with friends before his crucifixion, Jesus wanted to make sure his most important ideas and feelings were not forgotten. In these final words about friendship, Jesus demanded a lot from his disciples: follow my teachings, the source of our life together; to honor our relationship, you must build my community.

The unity of fellowship among Jesus and his followers witnessed to God's love. And so Jesus prayed in John 17, "As you, Father, are in me and I am in you, may they also be in us, so that the world may believe that you have sent me . . . I in them and you in me, that they may become completely one, so that the world may know that you have sent me and have loved them even as you have loved me." Often called Jesus's "high-priestly prayer," this important passage from John's Gospel shows how Jesus's union with God the Father was the glue that cemented his followers' relationships with one another—and with the rest of the world.

Usually when Christians think about mission, they turn to the Gospel of Matthew and cite the Great Commission in chapter 28, "Go therefore and make disciples of all nations," and the Great Commandment in chapter 22, "Love the Lord your God with all your heart, and with all your soul, and with all your mind," and "love your neighbor as yourself." Sharing the good news and serving one's neighbor are two of the chief ways of following Jesus Christ. But the Gospel of John introduces the relational implications of following Jesus—namely, love for specific persons who are the unique and beloved children of God. Human friendship inspires accountability to God and neighbor. Being friends with Jesus, within the worldwide community of faith, is a missional practice that witnesses to the reign of God. Jesus called this the "new commandment"—that his disciples love one another, just as he loved them (John 13:34).

Stan Skreslet notes that John is unique in showing how people came to follow Jesus through friendship with other followers. Many of Jesus's early followers were introduced to him by others. "Sharing Christ with friends," says Skreslet, "is what happens when followers of Jesus open up to loved ones or others with whom they are already in relationship and share their experience of faith in personal terms."[5] In the Gospel of John, Jesus's kingdom mission is spread through forming relationships. Donald McGavran calls people the "bridges of God" over which the good news spreads from one group to another,[6] and Alan and Eleanor Kreider note that "studies have indicated that friendship is the most important single force behind people becoming Christian."[7] The Gospel of John grounds that bridging function in friendships. Jesus approached others in love and humility. In knowing Jesus, people came to know God.

Jesus's Friendship Ethic

Of the many stories in the Gospel of John that reveal what Jesus meant by friendship, I will focus on three. Each of them models a spiritual aspect of relationships with others.

What Are You Looking For, and Where Are You Staying?

John 1:38–39 describes Jesus's calling of his first disciples: "When Jesus turned and saw them following, he said to them, 'What are you looking for?' They said to him, 'Rabbi' (which translated means Teacher), 'where are you staying?' He said to them, 'Come and see.' They came and saw where he was staying, and they remained with him that day."

When these two disciples met Jesus, the first thing they did was put down some roots. They spent time with Jesus. They located themselves in a deep spiritual relationship. When Jesus called them, their first task was to get to know him, and to share him with each other. The patience of remaining was the foundation of their friendship. Jesus's first question to them was, "What are you looking for?" And the answer was to find out where Jesus was staying so they could remain there with him.

The meaning of friendship in the Gospel of John is revealed in the author's repeated use of the verb *meno*, meaning to remain, stay, abide, live, or dwell. Of the 120 occurrences of the verb *meno* in the New Testament, well over half occur in the Johannine tradition. To remain, to dwell in relationship, represents the communion between Jesus and the Father, and thus between humanity and God. Through fellowship, Jesus's followers catch a glimpse of the great joy that awaits them in full, eternal communion with God. The verb *meno* occurs forty times in the Gospel of John.[8] Jesus's discussion of the grapevine and its branches in John 15 is all about the need for his followers to stay rooted in the vine by remaining embedded in relationship with him. Jesus says in verses 9–10, "As the Father has loved me, so I have loved you; abide in my love. If you keep my commandments, you will abide in my love, just as I have kept my Father's commandments and abide in his love."

The idea of remaining and abiding suggests Jesus's being fully present to his disciples, as well as the physical and psychological solidarity with humanity that characterizes the incarnation. To follow the way of Jesus Christ means engaging in the quality of relationship Jesus expected of his disciples: the friendship of remaining, of "abiding in the vine" through the changing seasons of life.[9]

Baptist leader Catherine Allen has shared a moving story she heard from Baptist women in Moldova. During the 1920s and 1930s, a missionary named Hazel Anna Craighead founded women's groups in the Baptist churches there. Through her friendships with women, Craighead mentored them for leadership. One of her protégés was Lydia Caldararu, the first woman selected for formal ministry by Baptists in that region. When the Soviet Communists began severely persecuting the churches and drove out the missionaries around 1939, Caldararu continued to minister underground among women's groups. She was captured, sentenced to death, and sent to Siberia for fifteen years. Baptist women leaders died in prison. And yet the women's groups remained faithful during fifty years of persecution. After the Iron Curtain was torn down in 1989 and the Soviet Union broke apart, "Anna" circles resurfaced in Moldova. Before she died, Caldararu passed on the leadership to young women she had secretly trained. Although the Baptist women of Moldova had forgotten the name of the missionary who inspired their women's groups, in the early 2000s they rediscovered who she was and began researching the stories of the faithful women who kept the Baptist church alive through women's groups in Moldova. Renewed relationships today between Baptist women in the US and Moldova were built on the foundation of the faithful friendship of remaining between Hazel Anna Craighead and Lydia Caldararu during the 1930s.[10]

And herein lies the paradox of remaining. To remain is often to be invisible where your very name is forgotten except by the people to whom you are the closest. Those who travel to and fro get more attention than those who commit to remaining in relationship with particular people. Anyone who has worked with children in groups like Boys and Girls Clubs or Foster Grandparents knows that consistency and regularity with the small acts of remaining is the key to love and growth. The spiritual lesson of the disciples remaining with Jesus is the promise of God's kingdom represented by the mustard seed: small, invisible acts of commitment are necessary for the growth and fullness of love, justice, and peace.

Friendship requires commitment both to Jesus Christ and to others unlike oneself, in concrete, specific, and long-term relationships. Peruvian mission leader Samuel Escobar has complained that instead of doing the hard work of interacting with local communities when abroad, Christian travelers often retreat to their homes in the evenings and email their friends back in the US.[11] It is easier to text or WhatsApp the people back home than to risk immersing oneself in unfamiliar social contexts that involve meeting and mingling with strangers. Americans think of themselves as friendly people, but they want friendship on their own cultural terms; they want familiarity with few real obligations. But Jesus asks, "What are you looking for?" And the answer is to be fully present, remaining with Jesus and with the people he asks his followers to love and to serve.

Give Me a Drink

Among Jesus's many deep encounters with people in the Gospel of John, one of the most surprising is his conversation with the Samaritan woman in chapter 4. Being from the northern province of Galilee, Jesus had to pass through Samaria to go home. He sat down by the well in Sychar. When a Samaritan woman approached, Jesus asked her for a drink. In that simple request, Jesus crossed the boundaries of gender, ethnicity, and religion. The woman's reaction was to say, "How is it that you, a Jew, ask a drink of me, a woman of Samaria?"

What is immediately noticeable about this passage is that Jesus sat down in the Samaritan woman's town and asked her for help. He entered into a relationship of mutual exchange by assuming that she had something to offer him. In cross-cultural outreach, especially to the poor, Americans usually focus on bringing in stuff to help others. But the surprising encounter with the Samaritan woman did not occur when a well-equipped squad of disciples descended on a needy Samaritan village. Here was Jesus himself, in a cross-cultural situation, and the first thing he did was to ask a local woman for help. His request for water, necessary for survival, opened the door to a mutual exchange between people who were not usually seen as equals. Jesus's request for water opened the door through which he entered the woman's reality. It led to a deeper exchange about the stuff of life—the "living water."

Jesus's request for a drink demonstrates the foundation of friendship, which is mutuality. One of the things I find the hardest when I go to rural Zimbabwe is to accept things from poor people. I want to remain in control by being the one who gives out things. Also, I feel guilty if I take food or gifts from the poor. But who am I to make the decision that they cannot afford to give me a gift? The mutuality of friendship requires being willing to receive.

My former pastor Scott Campbell tells the story of when he was a boy in rural Kentucky. His father was a minister, and the people in the church took turns every Sunday in inviting the pastor and his family over for lunch. One family in the church was very poor. They lived on a small farm and grew their own vegetables. They had almost no money. But they wanted to invite the minister's family over for Sunday dinner. So the minister's family drove to the hollow where the poor folks lived. They sat down for a meal of vegetables. Then the poor family proudly brought out a can of Spam, which had been carefully cut into slices and fried. Because the family could afford only one can, the pastor and his family had to eat the Spam while the poor family watched. Needless to say, the visitors did not wish to eat it—especially with the poor family watching them. But to have refused their hospitality would have been to refuse their friendship.

In asking the Samaritan woman for a drink, Jesus was opening himself to her reality. He became a listener and a dialogue partner, not an outsider who came to impose his own agenda on the Samaritan populace. The result of this unexpected relationship was that the Samaritan woman ran to share it with others in her village. The good news spread along a chain of relationships of knowing and being known. As Jesus showed in his conversation with the woman at the well, his mission required mutual vulnerability. In fact, in John 8:48, Jesus's critics accused him of being a Samaritan and of having a demon. Because of his risk-taking—his openness to the other—Jesus was accused of being a dangerous outsider himself.

The Japanese theologian Kosuke Koyama was a missionary for many years in Thailand. One of the insights he gained from his relationships there was the importance of what he called "neighborology." Being a neighbor meant accepting that even the poor had messages for him. Talking of God was meaningless unless he first engaged people on their own terms. Koyama cited 1 John 4:20: "He who does not love his brother whom he has seen cannot love God whom he has not seen."[12] Good neighborology, not theological abstractions, is the best way to convey the spirit of Christ. This follows the practices of Jesus, who was willing to break religious rules to heal on the Sabbath. In so doing, Jesus put his neighbor before abstract theology.

A stirring example of neighborology took place in September 2007. Between fifteen and twenty thousand protestors marched on the small town of Jena, Louisiana. Six African American youth had been convicted of assault against a white student. The trial occurred against a backdrop of growing racial tension, and the young men faced the prospect of long prison sentences. Some months earlier, several nooses were hung from the limbs of a large tree where teenagers often gathered to hang out. The situation of the young men, dubbed the Jena Six, awaiting their sentences attracted attention from around the world. Their trial was yet another example of the United States' violent history of unequal justice for African Americans.[13]

The largely white town of Jena, with a population of only three thousand, reacted with fear to the arrival of the mostly

African American marchers. On September 20, stores and the town hall remained closed. People hesitated to leave their houses ... except for the members of one church congregation. They erected a sign at the edge of town that proclaimed, "Open Hearts. Open Minds. Open Doors." Members of the largely white congregation arrived in their church parking lot at 7:00 a.m. to greet the marchers. Led by the pastor, the Reverend Lyndle Bullard, Nolley United Methodist Church opened its doors so that marchers could use the toilet and rest. Said Bullard, "We just started greeting people and finding out where they were from. We thanked them for coming and welcomed them to Jena. We talked about hospitality."[14]

A year after the peaceful demonstration in Jena, Rev. Bullard reflected, "I think the events of September 20 changed my church. . . . I think it scared them at first that we were opening up the church, but when nothing happened to the church and they came up and spoke to the people who came, it opened up their hearts. Wonderful is the only way I can describe it."[15]

In the months following the protest march, the clergy in Jena led efforts to help the townspeople search their hearts and make sure race and racism would not divide them in the future. The local paper commented, "Nearly everyone you talk to in Jena credits faith and religion for the community's evolution and ability to weather the storm that came with such events like the rally and the national media converging on Jena."[16] Early in 2008, what began as a one-week revival in a local church stretched into a nine-week event that drew hundreds of people nightly from the surrounding area and involved all the churches in town. The revival became the source of healing and reconciliation for the townspeople. People of different races and beliefs came together to worship and to share with one another. Rev. Bullard noted how the black and white ministers presented a united front and also held services of thanksgiving and interracial prayer meetings throughout the year.

In other concrete actions, one woman opened an internet coffee shop so youth would have a place to socialize after school. The tree from which nooses had been hung was cut down for the rebuilding of the high school, which had burned down earlier. Blacks and whites visited one another's porches and hugged when they saw each other at Walmart. The Department of Justice launched a special program for high school students to help them deal with racial issues. Churches throughout Louisiana prayed for "justice and healing" in Jena. In September 2008, African American Baptist pastor Jimmy Young summarized the spirit in Jena in the months after the revival: "In every city and state in this union, we have the problems we have here. . . . No legislation can be passed, no law made, to make people love one another. The only way is to change their heart through God. And that has happened here. I think we've done well. I think we took the right steps for the positive changes to take place."[17]

Faithful friendships that grew in Jena resulted from Christian people being vulnerable enough to ask each other, "What do you need?" or to say, "Give me a drink." It would be naive to think that neighborology solved all the racial problems in Jena, or transformed unjust systems. But through simple acts of offering and accepting hospitality, the community planted mustard seeds of hope. Growing interracial relationships built a bridge over which blacks and whites could travel together toward reconciliation.

Where Have You Laid Him?

Probably the deepest personal friendship explored in the Gospel of John is that of Jesus with Lazarus and his sisters Mary and Martha. Jesus often spent time in their home, eating and talking with them. In John 11, it reads that Lazarus got sick and died. By the time Jesus arrived, Lazarus had already been entombed for four days. The text says that when Jesus saw Mary and the mourners crying, "he was greatly disturbed in spirit and deeply moved. He said, 'Where have you laid him?' They said to him, 'Lord, come and see.' Jesus began to weep. So the Jews said, 'See how he loved him!'" (John 11:33-36).

This amazing passage shows Jesus crying in grief at the loss of a friend. He entered fully into the pain and sorrow of human life. He walked right into it, and through it. Even though he may have known what the onlookers did not—that Lazarus would soon rise from the dead—he accompanied the mourners in their distress. He did not use his divinity to avoid the pain of life. To have dismissed the pain of Mary and Martha, and to have failed to mourn Lazarus, would have been to deny his humanity. Jesus was not a docetic figure, above the fray of human suffering. When Jesus asked, "Where have you laid him?" he entered the depths of what it means to be fully human.

Jesus's friendship with Lazarus gives us another insight into the meaning of friendship. This is the solidarity of accompaniment. The words *accompany*, *compassion*, and *companion* come from the Latin root *com*, meaning "together." To truly accompany others in their daily lives, as we grow together in grace, requires entering their reality. It requires sharing grief, as well as the joys of worship, family meals, and children's activities. When North Americans go into other cultures, they often don't stay long enough to get beyond the ever-present smiles of the people. To walk beside people and to be their friend means doing it long enough to go beneath the smiles. This kind of incarnational friendship is hard work and not for everyone. Churches often talk about partnership—about mission partners, and shared project goals. But partnership barely scratches the surface. Friendship goes deeper than partnership. It requires asking, "Where have you laid him?" Like Jesus, his followers must cry and mourn with their suffering friends—and celebrate new life together as well.

In January 2010, a powerful earthquake struck Haiti, killing over three hundred thousand people and leaving a million people homeless. Mission and service groups already in service in Haiti were hard-hit. An American missionary named Jim Gulley was buried in a hole under the collapsed Hotel Montana for three days. The other two male mission colleagues buried with him in the hole died. And then, like Lazarus, Gulley was resurrected. French rescuers dug him out, along with another survivor. When I asked Jim how his life had changed by being buried under the Hotel Montana, he said not at all. Because in his decision to become a missionary years before, he was already prepared to suffer and to die with the people he went to serve.

Another moving example of sharing the pain of people's daily lives is that of the Maryknoll Sisters among the Japanese during the Second World War. The Sisters had begun working among the Japanese in California and Washington in 1920 and in Hawaii in 1927. They ran an orphanage and schools for the Japanese in Los Angeles. Because of racism and fear they would betray the United States, about 110,000 Americans of Japanese descent were herded into internment camps after Japan bombed Pearl Harbor. Japanese Americans left behind everything they owned, except for two suitcases, and moved into prisonlike barracks. Even orphans only one-eighth Japanese, and as young as six months, were deemed a risk to national security and were dumped into a desolate "Children's Village" in the Manzanar internment camp.

Two Japanese American Sisters, Mary Susanna Hayashi and Bernadette Yoshumochi, though allowed by law to remain outside, moved into Manzanar, as did other Maryknollers. There they ran a home and school for the orphans. From Seattle and Los Angeles, Maryknoll Sisters remained with their Japanese parishioners. After the close of this infamous example of American injustice, Japanese Catholics worked to restore the Maryknoll community in Los Angeles. Former Japanese internees continued to worship at the crumbling remains of their chapels, in solidarity with the Sisters who were in solidarity with them.[18]

"Where have you laid him?" In asking this question, Jesus showed his solidarity with his friends—with ordinary humanity. John writes that after Jesus raised Lazarus from the dead, many people believed he was the Messiah. Probably they believed in him because he raised Lazarus from the dead. But perhaps also they believed in him because he cried with them.

Conclusion: Sent Out in Friendship

In thinking about the humanity of Jesus, it is possible to envision him as a friend. After all, he walked, talked, ate, and did all the normal things that humans do. Jesus got hungry and ate at his friends' houses. He got tired, and tried to get away from the crowds to rest. He got irritated at people when they did not understand what he was talking about, and he got angry when people exploited the poor. He expressed appreciation, such as when a woman bathed his feet and wiped them with her hair. In the garden of Gethsemane, praying before he died, Jesus showed fear and regret, asking God to take away the burden of his own destruction. He also showed courage—promising to persevere to the end. And Jesus loved his friends.

Theologians have written many books about the different kinds of love expressed in the Gospel of John.[19] My purpose here is not to exegete the complex meanings of love in the Bible but rather to make the simple point that taking the human Jesus seriously requires paying attention to friendship as a biblical practice. To narrate Jesus's life is to see him within human relationships. Jesus's disciples experienced God through their intimacy with Jesus.

Of the many things the Gospel of John teaches about friendship, I have touched on three spiritual dimensions important for faithful relationships:

• What are you looking for, and where are you staying? Friendship involves being located in concrete relationship with Jesus and accountable to specific persons and places.

- Give me a drink. Friendship involves listening, sharing, and giving and receiving in mutuality.
- Where have you laid him? Friendship involves empathizing and suffering with others, including walking with them through the tough parts of life, such as illness and death.

The personal encounters between Jesus and his friends show that cross-cultural friendship is more than traveling to see new places. It is more than short-term projects to help the poor. Friendship in the way of Jesus is a matter of incarnational practice, of solidarity with and love for others.

If Jesus had been merely human, his friendships would have stopped with the crucifixion. His friends would have remembered him and reminisced about what it was like when they were together. They might have collected his sayings. Subsequent generations might have read stories about his relationships. But later generations could not have also claimed to be his friend.

Yet friendship in the way of Jesus did not stop with his death. The resurrection followed the crucifixion. Resurrected and glorified, Jesus returned to meet his friends. The Gospel of John is the testimony of the disciple whom Jesus loved (John 21:20-24). And this testimony contains multiple examples of the resurrected Jesus appearing to the disciples and interacting with them in human ways—eating, breathing, talking, being interested in fishing, and showing them his wounds.

Because Jesus rose from the dead, the meaning of friendship with him was transformed. It moved from the realm of human limitations to that of divine possibilities. It moved from the boundedness of a specific location and small circle of close friends to the sharing of stories of Jesus across boundaries of time and place. In John 20:19–23, in encountering the resurrected Jesus, the disciples renewed their relationship with him. Their friend and master dead, the fearful disciples were hiding behind locked doors. Jesus appeared and blessed them with the words "Peace be with you." He showed them his wounded body, and "the disciples rejoiced when they saw the Lord." From fear came joy. From abandonment came certainty. "Jesus said to them again, 'Peace be with you. As the Father has sent me, so I send you.' When he had said this, he breathed on them and said to them, 'Receive the Holy Spirit.'" Jesus appeared in person, and through the physical act of breathing, he sent out his disciples in peace. He also sent them out in relationship: "As the Father has sent me, so I send you." With the breath of Jesus warm upon them and the Holy Spirit to guide them, the disciples knew that their relationship with their friend, while no longer bound to the earth, was not over.

Through the resurrection, Jesus was revealed to be the Messiah, or what Greek speakers called the Christ. Thomas, who did not believe it at first, was also the first to proclaim this new understanding when he said, "My Lord and my God!" (John 20:28). Jesus's status as the Son of God marked a new stage in his disciples' relationship with him. But what did it mean for friendship?

In the "Friendship" chapter in *The Four Loves*, C. S. Lewis comments that while lovers look at each other, friends stand side by side. Friends stand beside each other because their eyes are fixed on what they have in common rather than on each other.[20] Friends have a common vision. They "see the same truth."[21] As Lewis says, "You will not find the warrior, the poet, the philosopher, or the Christian by staring in his eyes. . . . Better fight beside him, read with him, argue with him, pray with him."[22]

Lewis's comments can be applied to friendship in the wake of the resurrection. As the disciples remained fixed on the resurrected Jesus, their Lord and Savior, their faithfulness to one another deepened. The life of Jesus with his disciples was the beginning of an expanding network of relationships that has cascaded down through the ages. Standing side by side, the friends of Jesus are called to intimate relationship with the risen Lord and with each other.

CHAPTER 2

Cultivating Christian Friendship

Conversations through History

No man can do everything by himself, and so God commands friendship, so that we would help one another. Thus, if friendship were to disappear from this world, then the world would, without a doubt, come to an end.

—Matteo Ricci, *Treatise on Friendship*

What is friendship? This important question has engaged philosophers, theologians, writers, and poets from the time of the ancients to the present. The Chinese sage Confucius regarded friendship as a mutual relationship between equals and one of the sacred bonds that holds society together. Following Aristotle, the Latin philosopher and politician Cicero defined friendship as goodwill toward the beloved for one's own benefit, "reciprocated in equal measure."[1] The Greek biographer Plutarch wrote that "true friendship seeks after three things above all else: virtue as a good thing, intimacy as a pleasant thing, and usefulness as a necessary thing."[2] These classic and influential definitions of friendship agree on this: true friendship occurs between equals, it is shared rather than one-sided, and it encourages virtue that improves the individual person and undergirds an orderly society.

But the coming of Christianity challenged these definitions. The example of Jesus in relationship with his disciples added an important new dimension to classical understandings: for Jesus, love from and to God provided the basis for friendship among his followers. Instead of viewing friendship as an incubator of aristocratic male values, early Christians grounded it in the higher ideals and transcendent notion of a loving God.[3] Over the centuries, Christian notions of friendship expanded the boundaries of community. Christian community included women, slaves, working-class people, and others besides just the privileged male elites. The concept of *caritas*, love for God's sake, extended the possibilities of friendship to include potentially the whole world. In reflecting the universal love of God through Jesus Christ, love of God and love of neighbor could not be separated.[4]

English theologian Jeremy Taylor, in a popular treatise on friendship written in 1657, argues that even imperfect human friendships are a reflection of divine ones. Therefore, says Taylor, "Christians [have] a responsibility to form as many friendships as possible."[5] Following the spirit of Taylor, I assert that down through the ages, Christians have often felt the responsibility to make friends. Grounded in the love of God and the example of Jesus and the disciples, Christian ideals of friendship require continually reaching beyond oneself toward mutual relationships.

But the devil remains in the details. In a Christian framework, how does friendship between specific individual persons relate to the ideals of universal love in Christ? For the apostle Paul, for example, being a coworker in Christ was more important than being a personal friend. From a Christian perspective, should personal friendship be secondary to the well-being of local communities of faith? Does the love of Christ lead to friendships, or do friendships draw people into the love of Christ? If the fullness of Jesus Christ requires reaching across cultures, nations, genders, and ethnicities to befriend even those who reject the Christian messenger and message, what does that look like? Hard questions remain, especially when one thinks about building community across boundaries that normally divide people.

This chapter explores how some Christians in the past have tried to work through the complexities of being a friend to folks unlike themselves. It shows that defining Christian friendship is an ongoing conversation that cuts across the centuries and continues today. The three case studies explored here focus on both the discourse and the practices of friendship—that is, how changing definitions of Christian friendship lead to specific actions in different cultural contexts. The practices discussed do not necessarily satisfy contemporary understandings of friendship and what constitutes equal relationships. Yet cumulatively, these examples show that, in theory at least, followers of Jesus Christ cannot separate the love of God from love of others—even those unlike themselves in obvious ways.

Friendship as Cultural Bridge: Matteo Ricci, the Jesuits, and the Xu Family in China

One of the most important cross-cultural conversations about the meaning of friendship occurred in the late sixteenth and early seventeenth centuries. During that time, philosophies and practices of friendship were vitally important to Renaissance humanists, who explored ancient Greek and Latin philosophy and literature from the perspective of late medieval Christian theology. The 1300s to the 1600s had seen an explosion of works written on friendship, letters between friends, and the founding of "confraternities," small groups of laity who shared common spiritual goals.[6] In 1508, the Dutch scholar Erasmus published a collection of ancient Greek and Roman sayings, the first of which was a quotation from Pythagoras: "Friends hold all things in common." Thus by the time Italian Jesuit missionaries sailed to China in the 1580s, they took with them not only their training in philosophy, rhetoric, astronomy, mathematics, theology, and Greek and Latin texts, but also an interest in the relationship between friendship and the cultivation of virtue. Indeed, the founding of the Society of Jesus (the Jesuits) in 1540 was itself an example of friendship, as they were a "band of brothers" who committed themselves to Jesus, to the church, to intellectual and spiritual discipline, and to worldwide mission.

In the work of Matteo Ricci, the greatest of the early Jesuit missionaries in China, friendship was a key point of contact between different cultures.[7] China in the 1500s distrusted outsiders. For a foreigner to enter, much less live there, required permission from the highest ruling authorities. The emperor held absolute power, mediated through a politicized bureaucracy of eunuchs, scholars, and regional officials. With Portugal and Spain extending their empires throughout Southeast Asia, the Chinese suspected foreign priests of being enemies of the state. Yet through his philosophical writings, useful scientific knowledge, and practices of friendship, Ricci managed to bridge European and Chinese cultures. And across that bridge, knowledge of Asia spread to Europe, and knowledge of Europe, including Christianity, spread to China.

While still a student, Ricci dedicated himself to becoming one of the first Roman Catholic missionaries in China. He arrived in Asia in 1582 and immediately began studying Chinese. This task was incredibly difficult, given the lack of dictionaries and other linguistic tools. Ricci and his senior colleague Michele Ruggieri moved to China in 1583. The early Jesuits were tolerated by the authorities because of their great knowledge—especially of mapmaking, astronomy, and other scientific fields useful for the authority of the Chinese emperor. Finally, in 1601, Ricci was allowed into Beijing, the capital of the empire.

During the decades he spent studying and molding himself to Chinese ways of being, Ricci befriended Confucian intellectuals. He practiced constant hospitality, conversing with a steady stream of curious visitors. He became close friends with Qu Rukuei, a young scholar interested in learning from him about math and science. This relationship gave Ricci the insights he needed to become accepted as a Chinese scholar.[8] At the time of his death in 1610, Ricci left behind a Chinese Catholic Church that fit well with Confucianism, the reigning philosophical framework undergirding Chinese society. His respect for Chinese culture meant he was deeply respected himself, and the emperor allowed him to be buried in Beijing. Today Matteo Ricci is remembered as a pioneer of what is called "inculturation."[9] Though not yet an official saint, his cause is under consideration by the Vatican.

In addition to his huge personal capacity for friendships with Confucian intellectuals, a major breakthrough in Ricci's social status occurred in 1595, when he composed his first work in Chinese, *A Treatise on Friendship*. This work was immediately popular and eagerly republished by Chinese literati themselves.[10] Ricci's collection of wise sayings greatly appealed to Confucian scholars, for whom loyalty between friends was one of the main pillars of society, along with the father-son relationship. Ricci composed *Friendship* in response to "King" Chiengan Chienzai, a Ming prince, who asked him the views of the West about the subject. Ricci wrote in Chinese the aphorisms and philosophical wisdom dating back to his childhood in Italy and encompassing the classical Renaissance-era education he had received. The first adage echoes Aristotle: "A friend is nothing but my other half, or my other self. So it is necessary to treat a friend as he were yourself."[11] Many of Ricci's sayings resonated with Confucian culture, and they were copied extensively into Ming literature.

Ricci's sentences on friendship, however, deviate from both the classical and Confucian worldviews in one key respect: they uphold a relationship with God as paramount. Adage 16 reads, "No man can do everything by himself, and so God commands friendship, so that we would help one another. Thus, if friendship were to disappear from this world, then the world would, without a doubt, come to an end."[12] In this important adage, Ricci introduces the Christian concept of friendship, stating that God is behind friendship of people with each other. Friendship thus has a higher purpose than its own satisfaction. Friendship provides a basis on which people help each other. This God-given mandate for human friendship is so important that, in Ricci's opinion, the world would destroy itself without it!

Ricci's treatise on friendship opened the door to deeper personal friendships and to the good news of the "Lord of Heaven," Ricci's term for God in Chinese. Ricci's philosophical work on friendship gave him a firm foundation for relating closely to Confucian scholars, especially those who were frustrated at the stagnant rigidity of contemporary definitions of Confucianism. Ricci argued that Christianity was compatible with the teachings of Confucius himself rather than with the more recent accretions to Confucian ideas influenced by Buddhism. This compatibility meant that Christian ideas were an intellectually respectable position for some of Ricci's friends to adopt. And as they moved deeper into the mysteries of the Christian faith—its rituals, spiritual practices, and communal life—they began building the Catholic Church in China.

Ricci's relationship with his most famous friend, Xu Guangqi, shows how friendship moved from theory to practice to becoming a foundation for Catholicism in China. A famous drawing of Ricci and Xu shows them side by side, the same height, similarly dressed, with hands outstretched toward each other. Their pose is one of perfect equality and equilibrium: one on each side of an altar, with the cross in the middle and a portrait of the baby Jesus and his mother above it. In 1603, after reading Ricci's work on the meaning of God, Xu was baptized a Christian at age forty-one with the baptismal name Paul. He considered Ricci to be a "father figure."[13] To learn about Western science, he worked with Ricci as a translator of Confucian texts into Latin. Xu was the first Chinese translator of Western texts into Chinese, including works on geography, hydraulics, and Euclid's mathematics.[14] In his regular job as a government cabinet minister, he promoted modernization in both the military and agriculture, and closer collaboration with foreign scholars and cultural experts. From a secular perspective, Xu has been remembered as an outstanding scientist and agriculturist who improved life for the Chinese people. He was also the chief protector of the Catholic Church during his lifetime. For many years, he put his life and reputation on the line to defend the character and scientific work of the Jesuit priests and to prevent their deportation or execution. A deeply pious man, Xu traveled outside China twice to practice the Spiritual Exercises of Saint Ignatius of Loyola. A Jesuit missionary sat with him while he lay dying at the advanced age of seventy-one.

Xu argued that Christianity not only was compatible with Confucianism but that it also completed it. He set out his views of Christianity in a summary of doctrine:

> To place the service of God in the centre; to concern oneself with the salvation of the soul and the body; to attempt the way of filial piety and charity; to convert from one's own sins and to aspire to sanctity in order to enter the gates of Heaven . . . all of these teachings are part of a fundamental truth regarding Heaven and humanity. These teachings can render men more brotherly

and sincere, and stimulate to the highest degree their commitment to eradicating evil from their existence.[15]

For Xu, holiness, salvation, and human compassion were direct results of placing God at the center of life.

The friendship between the Xu family and the Jesuit missionaries continued into the next generations, especially through the charitable life and faith of Xu's granddaughter Candida. In upper-class Chinese society, women were not allowed much direct contact with the outside world, nor were they allowed to meet foreign men. Thus Xu Candida's life as patron of the Catholic Church was remarkable. She entered an arranged marriage to a non-Christian at age sixteen. By the time her husband died thirty years later, she had brought him and her household into Christianity. All eight of their children were baptized. As a righteous widow, Xu Candida spent the next thirty years organizing women to weave and embroider silk, sell it, and invest the money in the church. Her network of female friends and relatives worked alongside her. Like faithful widows since the days of the Roman Empire, she never remarried so that she could serve God. She employed a system of intermediaries who acted as her agents for charitable giving. Despite being cloistered at home according to social custom, she supported a truly astonishing range of causes, including buying four hundred Chinese books for the Vatican, founding an orphanage for abandoned children, financing dozens of Western missionaries, maintaining thirty-nine different churches, hiring blind storytellers to recite the gospel, embroidering sacred cloths and vestments, providing burials for the poor, and paying the expenses of confraternities.[16]

Xu Candida remained close to her Jesuit spiritual father, Philippe Couplet, who later wrote her biography. In 1680, a Jesuit missionary remained in her home for the last three days of her life and administered the last rites. Although gender and social norms would not permit the intimate friendship with Jesuits enjoyed by the men in her family, she nevertheless maintained ongoing relationships with the missionaries through intermediaries and Catholic spiritual practices. Her noble band of laywomen represented the power of friendship and devotion that made possible the church's outreach. The existence of small fellowship groups, and their leadership by celibate women (both virgins and widows), kept the Chinese church alive over long centuries of persecution and isolation from the West.[17]

During the 1600s, philosophies and practices of friendship shared by the Jesuits and Confucian scholars and their families bridged East and West. Friendship undergirded by faith in God stimulated outreach across generations, across genders, and between rich and poor Catholics in China. Personal friendship and compassionate human community walked hand in hand.

Friendship as Care for the Poor: Strangers' Friend Societies in Eighteenth-Century Britain and Ireland

The opposite condition of having friends is to be friendless. And throughout much of human history, being friendless was a death sentence. This condition was the case in the rapidly industrializing world of Great Britain in the late 1700s. Populations increased, the countryside grew overcrowded, and factories opened in urban areas. Whole families moved into cities like Manchester, Bristol, Dublin, and London, looking for work. With no government social safety net and no reliable medical care, the urban friendless—especially widows and the unemployed—crowded into slums, suffered starvation and nakedness, and died of infectious diseases like smallpox and scarlet fever. Tim Macquiban notes that during that time period, one-tenth of the population of London survived by begging.[18]

Changing social conditions left thousands of the working poor without the care of a church parish. Into this gap stepped John Wesley—Church of England priest, Oxford graduate, and outdoor evangelist. Because of the strict, "methodical" piety he practiced, including regular visitation to prisoners and the needy, Wesley and like-minded friends were slapped with the label "Methodists." Wesley and his traveling preachers spread across Great Britain, Ireland, and the Channel Islands. Their evangelical, "Arminian" message of God's grace carried a positive emphasis on holiness, self-discipline, and active good works that appealed to the growing middle classes of the era. Methodists met in small groups for spiritual accountability and mutual support. Their own experiences of rising up from poverty, with the help of spiritual friendships and hard work, made them especially attuned to the friendless, including the dislocated, foreigners, slaves, and women and children.

Thus in the late 1780s, close associates of John Wesley began founding what they called Strangers' Friend Societies in industrial cities. Volunteers organized themselves into committees that canvassed the slums, found "sick strangers," visited them, and relieved their needs over a period of weeks until they could get back on their feet. Strangers' Friend Societies collected donations of money and supplies such as blankets, clothing, and even work implements needed by the poor to make a living. The societies held fund-raisers and put out emergency appeals during crises. They opposed the system of debtors' prisons that locked up people who couldn't pay their debts, and they paid to get people out of debtors' prisons so they could work and earn money. In an era when the poor were told to be patient and content with their poverty,[19] the Strangers' Friend Societies stood out for their willingness to help people. The London Society's report for 1809 noted that its volunteer Visitors "do not make proselytes" and "don't care what sect or nation the persons belong to."[20] The Manchester Society noted that its focus was on "Sick Strangers, and such as have no helper."[21] In other words, fellow Methodists and those with obvious church affiliations were not eligible for aid. The motto of the movement, published on the front of its annual reports, was taken from Matthew 25:35–36: "I was an hungred, and ye gave me meat: I was a stranger, and ye took me in: naked, and ye clothed me: I was sick, and ye visited me" (KJV).[22]

By the early 1800s, the Strangers' Friend Society was the largest charitable agency in Great Britain. As Methodists emigrated to Australia and Canada, they set up Strangers' Friend Societies in their new homes. In an age before government care for the poor, the movement modeled systematic though temporary care through volunteers, many of them women. And the care was holistic. Not only did Visitors meet acute physical needs, but they also inquired after the spiritual and psychological needs of the desperately poor, many of whom were already dying by the time they were found. Interested children were enrolled in Sunday schools, where they could learn to read and get some support beyond what stressed-out parents could provide. Annual city reports of the movement recounted actual cases, cataloged the assistance given, and listed the names of subscribers/donors. In 1809, for example, London reported over twelve thousand individual visits the previous year and twelve pages of donors, most of whom gave about a pound sterling each (about eighty dollars today).[23]

Given that equality has always been a hallmark of true friendship, it is an important question whether relationships forged on charity can even be seen as friendship. What about the unequal power dynamics between a charitable Visitor and a dying poor family? What kind of reciprocity and mutuality can exist when one person gives and the other receives? The church visitors' movement has been justly criticized for the self-righteous attitudes and sense of superiority it sometimes represents. The urgent problem of how to relate to people across economic and class lines remains central to Christian outreach today.[24]

To understand how the people involved understood charitable friendship, all we have to go on is a few short paragraphs written from the perspective of the society Visitors. Even this brief description is remarkable in hinting at how real people felt about the real situations they faced. Case studies in the 1809 London report include that of an unemployed laborer named Charles Waters. Visitors described a desperate situation. The ill man with a wife and four children had to sell all their furniture and clothing to buy food. The wife of one of the official committee members visited their crowded room and was so disturbed by the condition of the family that she sent a blanket, coverings, and other things for them. Over a five-week period, as Waters lay dying, Visitors from the Strangers' Friend Society attended to and supported the family. During his illness, Waters "earnestly prayed for his benefactors."[25] And it seems his prayers were answered. For after he died, the society moved Waters's widow and children to better lodgings, gave them clothing and furniture, and found the widow a job working for several families connected to the society. The society report noted that the widow constantly praises God "for thus raising her up friends in a strange place among strangers, and earnestly prays for all who have administered to her necessities."[26] The friendship described in this case was marked by spiritual mutuality. Although the society Visitors were the ones giving money and goods, Waters and his wife reciprocated at a spiritual level by praying for them. While the brief story does not tell us that Waters's family became social equals with their better-off benefactors, it does indicate an ongoing relationship between Waters's widow and women connected with the society, who employed her in their homes so she could support her children. Personal relationships through Strangers' Friends Societies did not reflect the equality of social status assumed in classical definitions of friendship, nor do they conform to contemporary practices promoted by development agencies. But in their context, they demonstrated intimacy and respect within a shared commitment to the God of love.

The case of Thomas Evans describes the plight of a failed businessman with a wife and nine children, living in an unfurnished room with no beds or fresh air. The crowded conditions made the family ill, and the landlord harassed them for rent. The family were Christians and enjoyed praying with the society Visitors. In this case, the society found one particular donor who "greatly exerted himself on behalf of the poor family."[27] The benefactor clothed the family, provided their necessities, and found work for them. The father recovered and began working. Some of the children began attending a Sunday school. "The father lately called at the weekly meeting of the Strangers' Friend Society, with a grateful heart, and a cheerful countenance, to return thanks for the great benefits he had received."[28]

As with the Waterses, the case of the Evans family hints at deep personal commitment on the part of a devoted donor and mutual commitment by the poor. The attendance of children at Sunday school set up long-term interaction between the society and the family. In both cases, the suffering families moved from nearly dying friendless to having friends who helped them survive. Spiritual friendship extended in multiple directions.

Relationships between the Visitors and the urban poor was probably not what Americans in the twenty-first century think about when they hear the word *friendship*. But they do show how evangelical believers crossed boundaries of social class for the attempted betterment of humanity. John Wesley, the founder of Methodism, believed that works of mercy are a "means of grace" necessary to forming Christian character. Opening oneself to compassion, and empathizing with the poor and the needy, actually requires visiting them.[29] And visiting the poor is the starting point for potentially deeper mutual commitments. Friendship is nothing if not personal.

In correspondence with a Miss J. C. March, Wesley expressed his views on relationships with the poor. Miss March was wealthy. One of her hesitations to joining the Methodists had to do with the fact that so many of them were lower-class and therefore, in her opinion, lacked "good character." Wesley's response was to remind her that as a Christian, she lived on a higher spiritual plane. Therefore, she should go visit the poor. Jesus would be with her. And after all, she would be meeting the poor in heaven. The poor had more faith than the rich, wrote Wesley, and often "better taste."

> Go and see the poor and sick in their own little poor hovels. Take up your cross, woman! Remember the faith! Jesus went before you, and will go with you. . . . I want you to converse more, abundantly more, with the poorest of the people, who, if they have not taste, have souls. . . . And they have (many of them) faith and the love of God in a larger measure than any persons I know.[30]

When Miss March objected that she was incapable of befriending the poor, Wesley conceded that she need not go that far if she couldn't handle it, but that for the sake of her own holiness of character, she needed to visit them anyway. For John Wesley and his followers, love of God could not be separated from love of neighbor—and neighbors included the poor, the sick, and the stranger.

Friendship between Nations:
The 1920s World Friendship Movement and Japan

A century ago, of all the potential immigrants to the United States, none faced as much hostility as Asians. Following World War I, race relations sank to a new low. Despite economic recession in the United States, a flood of immigrants poured in after the war ended in 1918. Many were displaced persons from southern and eastern Europe, including a large number of Jews. Their presence evoked fear and hostility from the American-born population. Thus in 1921, the United States government enacted its first quotas for immigration restriction. It limited both the number and points of origin of new immigrants from Asia, Africa, and Europe. Then in 1924, the ax fell. New legislation not only severely limited immigration from "new" ethnic groups but also forbade all immigration of people who would not be allowed to become citizens anyway. And since Asians like Chinese and Japanese had long been restricted from gaining citizenship, the exclusion acts eliminated general immigration from Asia.

Before the Oriental Exclusion Act of 1924, relations between Americans and Japanese had been reasonably good.[31] Leading Japanese admired the United States. Since the late 1800s, Japan had undertaken a huge program of modernization. American missionaries to Japan were respected for having established modern schools and social services there. Although Japanese Christians were only a small percentage of the population, they were influential as social reformers and pro-democracy advocates. During a period of rapid industrialization and population increase, Japan was suffering a shortage of arable land. After 1894, Japanese farmers and laborers immigrated to Hawaii and California. As ethnic tensions grew in San Francisco, the two governments worked out a "gentlemen's agreement" in 1907 that restricted Japanese immigration but still allowed Japanese women to come as wives for those already present. Friendship was pledged between the nations, and in 1912 the mayor of Tokyo gave the mayor of Washington, DC, thousands of cherry trees that became a hallmark of friendship between the cities. Nevertheless, tension between the two countries continued to escalate over Japanese expansion in Asia and discrimination against Japanese in California. When the exclusion act of 1924 was passed, the Japanese felt deeply hurt and betrayed.

But countervailing trends existed. Sharing lifelong, solid friendships, some Japanese and American Christians had long acted as peace emissaries. For example, Japanese Quaker diplomat Inazo Nitobé and his American wife, Mary Elkinton, considered themselves "bridges across the Pacific." They supported Christian schools in Japan, and in 1911, to increase mutual respect between Japanese and Americans, the Carnegie Endowment for International Peace appointed Nitobé the first exchange professor from Japan to the United States.[32] Another peace emissary was Michi Kawai, a 1904 graduate of Bryn Mawr College, who returned to Japan to found girls' schools. She cofounded the Japanese Young Women's Christian Association and in 1912 became its first Japanese general secretary. Deeply committed to cross-cultural friendship, Kawai spent six months in the United States in 1910, telling Americans about the work of the YWCA in Japan and raising funds. She taught Japanese women, most of them "picture brides" matched by their parents to Japanese immigrant laborers, what to expect from life in the United States.[33]

Upon returning from Japan, some missionaries defended the rights of the Japanese in the United States. One of the most active of these was Sidney Gulick, who in 1886 began a quarter century of missionary work in Japan. Anti-Asian racism deeply concerned American missionaries in Asia and undercut their witness. In 1884, every Protestant missionary in southern Japan signed a public statement asking for revision of unequal treaties between the countries. In 1905, Gulick defended Japanese public policy and culture. To counter American hostility toward the so-called "yellow peril," he wrote about the "white peril" of aggression against East Asians. In 1911, he worked with the America-Japan Society to make possible the first faculty and student exchanges between Japan and the United States. He hoped that cultural exchanges would diminish prejudice against Japanese immigrants as well as assist in teaching English to Japanese. In 1913, Gulick returned to the United States and began working with the Federal Council of Churches on American immigration policy. He articulated his new role as a form of reverse mission: "I am as truly a missionary working for Japan as if I were in Japan."[34]

The situation in California was dire. Already Asians were ineligible for citizenship, and the California Alien Land Act of 1913 stripped them of their right to purchase agricultural land. Gulick responded to this crisis with his book *The American Japanese Problem: A Study of the Racial Relations of the East and the West*[35] and a speaking tour sponsored by Andrew Carnegie, the industrialist who was using his fortune to fund peace movements. Gulick improvised multiple ways to impact public opinion, including writing, incessant public speaking, and lobbying government officials. As a firm believer in universal Christian brotherhood, he placed his efforts within the framework of building world peace. Gulick was a founding member of the World Alliance for Promoting International Friendship through the Churches. The interdenominational group was holding its first international meeting in Germany when World War I broke out in August 1914. It advocated peacemaking and disarmament, supported conscientious objection and minority rights, and looked ahead in hope to a day when conflicts between nations would be handled by arbitration rather than war. During the First World War he traveled the country founding Peace Makers' Committees in local congregations.

Gulick's most successful action to support Japanese-American relations was allying with Protestant church women during the 1920s. After the devastation of World War I, leaders of the women's missionary organizations in Protestant denominations started using the term *world friendship* to describe their mission spirituality. In a world of war, colonialism, racism, and ethnic divisions, "world friendship assumed that western culture no longer had a monopoly on virtue, and that women around the world stood poised to lead their own people not to western Christian civilization, but to their own forms of Christian life."[36] What missions needed was partnership and friendship, not paternalism. Mainline Protestant women's missionary organizations—Methodists, Presbyterians, American Baptists, Disciples, Congregationalists, Lutherans, Episcopalians, and Reformed—argued that making friends across national and ethnic boundaries would lead to peace. This idea was also popular among college students. In the mid-1920s, mission clubs at many colleges changed their names to "World Friendship" clubs. In 1923, Methodist women's mission societies adopted world friendship as their mission focus for the 1920s. Representing the largest denominational group of mission volunteers in the country, the official move by Methodist women was very influential. Summarized one mission leader, "World Friendship is a new name for what has been in the hearts of missionary women from the beginning."[37]

Another important commitment to world friendship was the women's missionary tradition of the World Day of Prayer. The united practice of missionary women spending a day of intercessory prayer on behalf of foreign missions dated back to 1912. But in 1927, the combined Protestant women's mission boards adopted the practice of an annual World Day of Prayer. This ongoing, now international, movement believes that praying with other Christian women around the world on the same day is essential for spiritual friendships, for bridging national and ethnic differences, and for encouraging world peace. Writers of the prayers rotate among different countries, thereby encouraging women around the world to pray for one another.

In 1926, Sidney Gulick launched his most creative effort to improve ordinary Japanese-American relationships when he founded the Committee on World Friendship among Children. He searched for a point of contact between ordinary Japanese and ordinary Americans. He decided to introduce Americans to the Japanese festival of dolls, an annual celebration of the well-being of children during which people display dolls. Church women committed to world friendship facilitated the project. The committee taught American children about the Japanese festival. It got youth groups and schools to purchase and outfit American dolls as "messengers of good will and friendship."[38] A dollar each purchased "passports" for the dolls, which were sent to Japan for distribution to Japanese schools. Critics of Gulick's friendship doll exchange believed it was a colossal waste of time because it was incapable of dismantling racist systems, stopping wars, or correcting economic injustices. But on a popular level, this highly successful program resulted in Americans sending nearly thirteen thousand friendship dolls to Japan.[39] Japanese children responded by collecting money to send to the United States fifty-eight large Japanese dolls, beautifully outfitted in unique kimonos, with human hair, accompanied by full accessories and friendship letters. Named as representatives of Japanese cities, the Japanese dolls toured the country and then were distributed to museums in every state for display as gifts from the children of Japan to the children of America.[40] The magazines of women's mission groups promoted the project and its follow-up projects to children in Mexico and the Philippines.

Sadly, the world friendship movement of the 1920s was unable to reverse anti-Asian legislation in the US. After the bombing of Pearl Harbor, the Japanese friendship dolls were put into storage, or turned with their faces to the wall for the duration of the Second World War. In Japan, most of the dolls sent by American children were destroyed, but some were hidden away by their owners. The United States cleared the Japanese from California and interned 120,000 Japanese in prison camps. But as anyone who has enjoyed the Japanese cherry trees in Washington, DC, knows, hope for peaceful friendship springs eternal. Old or destroyed cherry trees in both Japan and Washington, DC, are replanted using cuttings from each other in order to continue the genetic stock of the original gifts and to symbolize friendship through the generations.

The story of the Japanese friendship dolls gives only a glimpse of the world friendship movement of the 1920s. Many ordinary church people longed to reach across national boundaries and make friends with people unlike themselves. Some pushed beyond racial stereotypes and welcomed international students, or donated money for international schools, or lobbied government representatives to change discriminatory laws against immigrants. It is impossible to tell how far friendship dolls transformed individual attitudes. But in an age before television, when overseas travel was rare, a child's sending a doll to Japan, or seeing "Miss Tokyo" or "Miss Yokohama" on tour, forged a physical link with people on the other side of the world. Friendship dolls humanized the "other." The dolls meant a lot to the children of the 1920s. After the Second World War, people in both Japan and the United States remembered them. They tried to find, rescue, and restore the surviving dolls—tangible artifacts of widespread hopes for international peace. The discourse and practices of world friendship, as idealistic as they were, embodied an enduring desire for human equality and world peace.

Conclusion: Christian Friendship in History

These case studies have illuminated three important moments in history when the Christian language of friendship was combined with concrete practices to cross boundaries that normally separate people.

- In sixteenth- and seventeenth-century China, friendship bridged cultures by connecting European Jesuit missionaries with Chinese intellectuals, who then reached out to other Chinese.
- In eighteenth-century Great Britain and Ireland, evangelical Protestants attacked the problem of urban industrial poverty by assisting and befriending needy strangers who lacked the resources for survival.
- In the United States in the early twentieth century, Protestant church leaders cultivated world friendship to challenge racial stereotypes and oppose discrimination against Asians.

Conversations across history about the meaning of cross-cultural friendship reveal a few common threads. In each case where the language of friendship was used, Christians were longing to make friends with people seen as unlike themselves. In all cases, the love of God and the love of humanity could not be separated. Indeed, the foundation of Christian friendship was not only the self-satisfaction of the individual friend but the desire to be faithful to Jesus's message of love. In so doing, Christians tried to make the world a better place.

Obviously none of these demonstrations of friendship was perfect. From today's vantage point, we can criticize them as inadequate to the gigantic social problems they tried to tackle. Nevertheless, ideals and practices of Christian friendship gave people hope. They were a concrete way that people tried to follow Jesus and reach out beyond themselves in difficult circumstances. Faithful friendship was holistic. It united spiritual yearnings with specific actions to share the faith, help the poor, and make peace in the world. The deeper meaning of these friendship movements is measured in human lives, whose names are now mostly lost to history. Like a stone dropped in a pond, each movement of friendship rippled outward. Ripple upon ripple revealed growing visions of diverse, peaceful, and loving human community. As Matteo Ricci put it, "If friendship were to disappear from this world, then the world would, without a doubt, come to an end."[41]

CHAPTER 3

"God with Us"

Friendship and Remaining

God is friend.

—Caroline Macdonald

The certainty of Emmanuel, "God with us," anchors Christian friendship. Through deep relationships with other persons, the presence of God becomes concrete and tangible. At its best, friendship communicates the unshakeable love of God through life's most challenging circumstances. The transitions of life and death, illness, social dislocation, and just the ordinary struggles of daily life can be transformed through the presence and prayers of friends. And if these friends are from another culture or ethnic group, the meaning of "God with us" deepens.

This chapter explores cross-cultural friendships as a dimension of remaining. In the relationships profiled here, people crossed barriers of culture, ethnicity, or nationhood to live in solidarity with others they weren't even supposed to know. They took up the long-term challenge of committing themselves to real people in real places, in the name of Christ. Through the witness of such friendships, "God with us" became a tangible reality for people on both sides of cultural or ethnic divides.

The first story introduces Caroline Macdonald, a Canadian missionary whose theology of "God as friend" challenged her to befriend Japanese prisoners and their families. The second example traces the inspiring friendship between Indian missionary Savarirayan Jesudason and Scottish Presbyterian Ernest Forrester-Paton as they lived in community together. Then finally comes the moving story of Dr. Yu Enmei, a Chinese Christian doctor whose friendship with American foreign missionaries resulted in her imprisonment for twenty-seven years. In all three cases, deliberate decisions to remain in fellowship with particular people embodied God's presence not only for those in relationship but for others around them.

God as Friend: Caroline Macdonald
and Prison Reform in Japan

When Caroline Macdonald died of lung cancer in 1931 at the age of fifty-six, she was wearing a small Japanese copper coin on a chain around her neck. Her biographer Margaret Prang narrates the long road to the remarkable relationship that lay behind that coin.[1]

A Canadian Presbyterian, Macdonald was one of the first female graduates of the University of Toronto. Her father was a medical doctor and a member of Parliament, and her mother had founded the local branch of the Presbyterian Woman's Foreign Missionary Society. While at the university, Macdonald worked in the YWCA, a Christian organization that helped young working women and college students. She arrived in Japan as a YWCA secretary in 1905, during the Russo-Japanese War. She remained there until she was diagnosed with cancer, returning to Canada two months before Japan invaded Manchuria. Macdonald's twenty-five years in Japan were marked by a highly unusual ministry of friendship, supported by her conviction that "God is friend."

From their beginnings in the 1850s through World War II a century later, relationships between Westerners and Japanese remained subject to the capricious swings of government policies and popular hostility against foreigners. In 1853, when the American admiral Matthew C. Perry sailed into Edo Bay and demanded that Japan open its ports to foreign trade, Christians had been severely persecuted in Japan already for 250 years. The Meiji Restoration of 1868 ushered in a program of modernization in which Western advisers, including missionaries, were welcome as educators. As Japan grew increasingly confident in its own global footprint, especially after it defeated Russia in 1905 and conquered Korea, its need for Westerners diminished. The widening path of militarization through the Second World War put cross-cultural relationships under a darkening cloud.

But notable cross-cultural friendships remained. Both the YMCA and YWCA, as they expanded into Asia, were known for their interracial teams of workers. Thus Macdonald worked closely with Michi Kawai and other Japanese women colleagues to establish the women's service organization.

Because of her leadership ability, she was chosen to be an official YWCA observer at the World Missionary Conference in Edinburgh in 1910.[2] She stayed in Scotland to study theology for a few months with theologian David Cairns and was the only woman in the Aberdeen theology school. Macdonald developed a strong theology of the kingdom of God, whose principles of equality and justice guided her active ministry.

Close personal relationships characterized Macdonald's ministry from the beginning. As part of her YWCA work, she ran Bible classes for both women and men. She also collaborated with Japanese Christian leaders such as her own pastor, the famous Reverend Uemura Masahisa. In partnership with Japanese Christian women educators, she ran summer conferences to train women leaders.

Tragedy struck in 1913 when Yamada Zen'ichi, a member of her Bible study class for two years, murdered his wife and two children. Macdonald felt personally responsible for the tragedy. She had not realized he needed help and had been too busy to see him. She and his friends held an all-night prayer vigil. She went through the challenging and time-consuming process of visiting Yamada in prison, sitting through the trial, and finding him a lawyer. She prepared him spiritually for the trial. He confessed and repented of the crime. That Yamada escaped the death sentence was due in no small part to Macdonald's bringing Yamada to the spiritual place of full repentance and seeking God's forgiveness, a factor the sentencing judge took into consideration. And so began Macdonald's new life of spending most of her time visiting prisoners and caring for their families. She quickly learned of the horrors of the Japanese prison system and the humiliation that prisoners and their families suffered on a daily basis because they were considered outcasts by Japanese society.

In 1915, Macdonald resigned her position with the YWCA and started raising support from Canadian Presbyterian women for a freelance prison ministry. Given the outbreak of World War I in 1914, she embarked on her "faith mission" at a particularly challenging time for fund-raising. She partnered with Japanese friends to agitate for a juvenile justice system. After traveling to New York to learn about modern criminology and prison reform movements, she returned to Japan equipped to press for more humane treatment for prisoners. Thousands of prisoners from across the country wrote her letters. A big part of her ministry was answering those letters and providing encouragement and support for individual prisoners. Much of their worry revolved around Japanese society's poor treatment of their wives and children.

To assist released prisoners in reuniting with their families, she developed a settlement house in East Tokyo. The settlement house movement had spread across the United Kingdom and North America as a way of remaining among the urban poor. Middle-class Christians moved into shared housing in the slums to live among the poor and to provide them community services, support, and especially friendship. After Japanese Christian social worker Toyohiko Kagawa started his settlement house in the Kobe slums in 1909, the movement spread in Japan.[3] Macdonald took in prisoners after their release, including many juveniles. She knew Kagawa, and she advised younger missionaries who worked in settlement houses.

As part of her prison ministry, in 1916, Macdonald sent special New Year's Day rice to Tokichi Ishii, who was famous for his many crimes and long years behind bars. She then sent him a Bible and spiritual books. Ishii had recently learned that another man was going to be hanged for the murder of a geisha girl whom Ishii himself had actually murdered. After struggling with his conscience, Ishii confessed to three murders. He worried about the fate of his own soul after death, especially now that he faced the death penalty. Ishii entered into a friendship with Caroline Macdonald and her missionary partner Annie West.[4]

Macdonald began supporting Ishii with frequent visits, presence at court appearances, and spiritual counseling. As he read the New Testament she gave him, he was struck by Jesus's words "Father, forgive them, for they know not what they do." Ishii later wrote of his experience:

> I stopped: I was stabbed to the heart, as if pierced by a five-inch nail. What did the verse reveal to me? Shall I call it the love of the heart of Christ? . . . I do not know what to call it. I only know that with an unspeakably grateful heart, I believed. Through this simple sentence I was led into the whole of Christianity.[5]

After receiving the death sentence for his confessed murders, at Macdonald's encouragement Ishii wrote down his life story and how he was transformed by his new relationship with Jesus Christ. He was executed in 1918, leaving Macdonald all his possessions: the manuscript and a copper coin. For the rest of her life, she wore the coin on a chain around her neck.[6] Ishii's final words before his execution were a poem:

My name is defiled
My body dies in prison
But my soul, purified
Today returns to the City of God.[7]

After her transformative friendship with Tokichi Ishii, Caroline Macdonald's commitment to prisoners deepened. She mentored them and social activists alike, many of whom became Christians. She was known for treating people equally and nurturing a wide network of Japanese friends. She promoted prison reform and comforted and supported the families of workers on strike. She corresponded with hundreds of prisoners and hosted visitors night and day—newly released prisoners, the families of prisoners, guards, and others desperate for help. She spent time with prisoners about to be executed. Her approach to the kingdom of God was reflected in her saying that "to save one soul is a step toward saving the whole world."[8] To the end of her life, she combined a robust theology of the kingdom of God with the missional practice of cross-cultural friendships with her adopted people, the Japanese.

Any woman as strong-minded as Caroline Macdonald was bound to be controversial for her generation. She was highly critical of Western missionary societies. She was an ardent feminist and supported women's education, and she was an active labor organizer. Most surprising for her era, she came out publicly in favor of interracial marriage. When in 1920, under the urging of her pastor, Uemura Masahisa, the Japanese Presbyterian Church decided to ordain women as elders, she was one of the first selected by her local congregation.

Macdonald was given a high award by the emperor of Japan and was the first woman to receive an honorary doctor of laws from her alma mater, the University of Toronto.

In summing up Macdonald's life, biographer Margaret Prang concludes,

> While Macdonald's intelligence, education, and spirit of adventure all shaped her life, the definitive factor in her unusual career was her great capacity for friendship. This was rooted in her deep conviction that social and cultural differences were to be respected but were ultimately of little importance. For her the essential reality was that "human nature is all one." It was no accident that her favorite metaphor for God was "Friend." Friendship was crucial to Caroline's achievement in the world and it was also her personal nourishment, taking the place of immediate family.[9]

Macdonald's capacity for friendship was expressed in her insistence that foreigners become fluent in Japanese and that they not criticize Japanese culture. She wrote, "We who call ourselves Christians have no reason for talking about the differences among us. Any fool can see the differences. It takes a loving heart and a well balanced head to see that we are all one. The likenesses are fundamental, the differences are superficial."[10]

Macdonald died of lung cancer shortly after returning to Canada. Her relationships with death-row Japanese prisoners had shed light on the terrible conditions in Japanese prisons and thus encouraged prison reform. At her funeral, governor of prisons Arima Shirosuke asked why a foreign woman had "chosen to be the friend of villains" whose own countrymen considered them to be "snakes and savage beasts." The answer, he concluded, was her faith, which caused her to treat every person as a child of God, regardless of "religion, race, or class."[11]

Faithful friendship is like the mustard seed of Jesus's parable. Although it is hard to trace out specific historical results from particular relationships, it is remarkable that Macdonald's friends and protégés read like a who's who of Japanese social reformers. After World War II, several of her protégés became the highest-ranking Christians in the Japanese government, including a supreme court judge, a speaker of the house, and a prime minister, and several helped found the Social Democratic Party.

Remaining in Community:
Savarirayan Jesudason and Ernest Forrester-Paton

Colonialism—and the racism that accompanied it—was probably the biggest obstacle to embracing diversity in the first half of the twentieth century.[12] And nowhere was European colonialism as entrenched as in India. In 1858, when the British officially took over the Indian subcontinent, they had already been in power for a century through the British East India Company. After World War I ended in 1918, India expected to gain its independence—especially after well over a million Indian volunteers supported the British Empire against the Germans. Instead, Indian soldiers returned home to even harsher British control. On April 13, 1919, a British general and troops massacred several hundred people. Following the Amritsar Massacre, the Indian independence movement exploded into action. Mahatma Gandhi and the Indian National Congress led boycotts, strikes, and other mass protests to persuade the British to leave India. In the 1930 Salt March alone, the British arrested sixty thousand peaceful protesters. It took decades of struggle and another world war before India (and Pakistan) became independent in 1948.

The power imbalance and racial prejudice embedded within the colonial mind-set, and underlined by the ancient caste system, meant that even educated Indians were treated like second-class citizens in their own country. In his 1924 novel *A Passage to India*, E. M. Forster wrote about the impossibility of true cross-cultural friendship as long as the British controlled India. And yet, even in this troubled context, some exemplary friendships occurred. One of the most remarkable was that between two medical missionaries: the Indian Savarirayan Jesudason and the Scot Ernest Forrester-Paton. Their friendship spanned two world wars, the nationalist Indian struggle for independence, and twenty years beyond independence. It ended only with their deaths—Jesudason's in 1969 and Forrester-Paton's a year later. They saw their cross-cultural, transnational friendship as a deliberate Christian witness against colonialism and racism, and a statement of hope in building the kingdom of God. In 1921, they founded the Christukula ("Family of Christ") Ashram in Tirupattur, Tamil Nadu. This experimental intentional community was based on the model of a Hindu family-like community with a shared spiritual life, combined with the traditions of Christian monasticism and the public service ethic of a Protestant mission station.

Savarirayan Jesudason was from a Tamil-speaking Christian family. As a child, he was sensitive and religious. He longed to be like Saint Francis of Assisi. He actively sought out people of other races and religions to befriend and with whom to talk about Jesus Christ. In his memoirs, he describes himself as a "black" man who suffered discrimination, even as a medical doctor. He faced racial prejudice from British teachers, Anglo-Indian students, and ordinary British travelers. With his devout Christian upbringing, he chafed at the gap between colonial racism and biblical principles, and he searched for like-minded people with whom to witness to Christian principles of human equality. Thus, on the boat over to Scotland to undertake medical training, he made friends with people from different nationalities. In 1911–12, he wrote to these friends and asked their opinion of "starting a world brotherhood transcending all narrow race, language, or colour barriers, accepting only one race, the race of humanity, the race of Him Who called Himself 'The SON OF MAN.'"[13]

While working as a doctor with the London Medical Mission, Jesudason met the Scottish Presbyterian medical student Ernest Forrester-Paton, a Cambridge graduate from a well-to-do mill owner's family. Forrester-Paton belonged to the Student Volunteer Movement for Foreign Missions and was befriending international students as he prepared for missionary service. He and Jesudason fellowshipped at the East and West Hostel of the Student Christian Movement in Hampstead, London, founded to bring British, Chinese, and Indian students together in friendship. They discovered "growing in us both a strange longing for friendship with members of other races as we met a few of such and began to realise something of the supra-national character of the Kingdom of God."[14] As Jesudason recalled, "We opened our hearts to each other and helped each other through prayer and fellowship. Thus as we shared our ideals and aspirations together, our hearts were knit into a very intimate friendship."[15] By March 1915, they had decided to work together in India. "Drawn together as friends and finding much in common in our ideals and struggles in life," they affirmed, "we desired to share as much as possible with one another, and so shortly after this it was arranged that we should both live and work together."[16]

But World War I almost destroyed their dreams. Both men were pacifists. Forrester-Paton barely escaped being imprisoned as a conscientious objector. Therefore, they accepted a missionary appointment to staff a mission hospital in Poona (Pune), India. Even in India, Forrester-Paton risked being drafted. He and Jesudason also faced the colonial racial hierarchy. The senior missionary pulled Forrester-Paton aside and told him that as a white man, he needed to be the head of the hospital. This he refused. The friends had agreed that foreigners should not boss Indians—not to mention that Jesudason was both older and a more experienced doctor. The friends determined to live beyond the assumption of white Western superiority. They got permission to live in a modest bungalow on the premises of the hospital instead of in the isolated mission compound. Besides running the hospital, they founded satellite clinics that they reached by bicycle. In contrast to the usual missionary designation of non-Western Christians as members of "younger churches," they adopted nicknames that confirmed Jesudason's seniority as "older brother" and Forrester-Paton's subordinate position as "younger brother."[17]

After jointly running the mission hospital in Poona and getting additional medical certifications in the United King-

dom, in 1921 they founded their ashram.[18] They allied themselves not with a hierarchical Western missionary agency but
with the "native" National Missionary Society. By founding
their own community, they could also choose to live in equality while they served the poor of the region. Forrester-Paton's
mother was their biggest supporter. Jesudason recalled that
she treated him like one of her own sons, approved of their
relationship, and addressed letters to them as "My dearest
boys."[19] When Forrester-Paton received a large inheritance
from his father, his mother approved of his giving away a
large part of it and then using the rest as the common purse
for the ashram. Thus Forrester-Paton's inheritance was the
financial foundation for their intentional community. It en-
abled them to outfit their hospital and school for the poor and
to give away their medical services for free or for a voluntary
donation. They tried to abolish caste and class distinctions
by relying on an all-volunteer force of workers. College and
seminary students often "tried out" the ashram during school
vacations or by participating in internships there for ministry
preparation. A stream of foreign missionaries also entered
the ashram for periods of time ranging from a few weeks to
a few years.

The older brother and younger brother were not the only
ones to found a Christian ashram in the 1920s. But theirs
was the most vigorous and successful of the early ones. Because celibacy was at the heart of their spiritual discipline,
they never recruited more than a handful of other permanent
members, though many came for short-term residencies. In a
speech he made at the Kotagiri missionary conference in 1925,
Forrester-Paton described the "three pillars" of the ashram:

"We came to conceive of a family of the followers of Christ living together and seeking to draw their fellowmen into vital touch with Christ by, first, a life of prayer and dependence upon God, secondly, love one to another, and thirdly, a life of selfless service."[20] The first pillar was reflected in the daily rhythm of the ashram. Every morning began early with private prayer and Bible study, followed by community worship and breakfast together. Evening worship, including the singing of Indian hymns, closed the day.

Love for one another, expressed in daily practices, was the second pillar. Jesudason noted, "Now no fellowship or friendship could be made to order. It must be a growth through loving personal intimacy. I am learning more and more that the secret of true and lasting fellowship is the secret of (or rather the grace for) forgiving one another."[21] Loving fellowship included practices of economic equality, in which personal needs were provided from the common fund and major expenses agreed by consensus.[22] Ashram residents dressed in simple, white Indian homespun cloth. This was the garb of the nationalist struggle, as modeled by Gandhi. The choice of clothing was political in the sense that it signified the equality of Western and Indian participants, and it affirmed Indian culture and economic integrity.

The third pillar of service was to witness to Christ's kingdom. In concrete terms, the outreach at Christukula Ashram began as medical work. Jesudason and Forrester-Paton were equipped to perform a wide range of surgeries, correct eye problems, and practice general medicine. They opened a hospital that at first housed twenty to twenty-five patients and then grew larger. Village schools were another form of social service provided by ashram participants, as was helping villagers better their living standards through improved agricultural production and hygiene.[23] Over time, other forms of service grew from the initial focus on medical work. In the context of the ongoing struggle for Indian independence, Jesudason explained the kingdom ideals of the ashram fellowship as "the unity of conflicting races in Christ," as well as the abolition of war and the caste system, education and social services for the masses, and cultivation of Indian leadership.[24]

By creating a spiritual family at Christukula Ashram, Jesudason and Forrester-Paton merged East and West and linked South Indian culture to the Christian longing for universal community. Both men spoke about their friendship at gatherings of the Student Christian Movement in the United Kingdom and India, and Forrester-Paton wrote the following in the organization's magazine, *The Student World*:

> We have been earnestly seeking to express our life and service in this Ashram in a way that will make Christianity more intelligible to the people of India, where, for so long, a deeply foreign tinge has been given to it, both in the churches and in the lives of the Christians. We have also been trying to bring about a home and a fellowship into which men called of God from other lands can come to India, not in the patronising attitude of teachers and leaders, but in humility seeking to learn and to serve along with Indian brothers, as well as to impart to others what they have been taught of God.[25]

The witness of Savarirayan Jesudason and Ernest Forrester-Paton embodied multiple kinds of remaining. First, of course, was their deep spiritual personal friendship and its lifelong outworking in intentional Christian community, a Family of Christ that welcomed members of different races and social classes. Second, the Christukula Ashram required remaining in one place over a lifetime. Serving their neighbors over many decades grounded their faith in the kingdom of God. The people of the villages near the ashram talked of it, with its hospital and schools, as coming down from heaven to bless them. As he reflected in later years on what the ashram meant to the people, Jesudason summed it up as "the creation of a fellowship of personalities that would put up 'a Jacob's ladder' pitched between Heaven and Tirupattur."[26] As in John 1:51, where Jesus prophesies that the angels of God would be seen ascending and descending on the Son of Man, "so must this 'ladder' be set up wherever Christ's faithful disciples unite their lives together to establish His kingdom on this earth."[27]

As part of remaining with the Indian people, the two friends committed themselves both culturally and politically to the people of India. Their holistic approach nurtured the intersection of Christian faith, Tamil culture, and the Indian struggle for full nationhood. Christukula Ashram experimented with building in South Asian temple styles, and as part of making Christ present to the people in Tamil Nadu, Jesudason became a well-known writer of Tamil Christian lyrics, which he set to traditional rhythmic melodies.[28] Jesudason and Forrester-Paton naturally supported India's independence as part of their commitment to racial equality. Jesudason saw no contradiction between his Christian faith and his patriotism. And in 1932, Forrester-Paton was arrested for "picketing" and beaten by police for participating in one of Gandhi's peaceful protests against British rule.

By remaining in Tirupattur and building their "Jacob's ladder" there, the Indian older brother and Scottish younger brother influenced the very missionary movement that in earlier years had tried to impose on them its Western racial hierarchy. In 1938, Jesudason attended the two-week-long International Missionary Council meeting in Madras, India, at the invitation of the chairman. Occurring every ten years, this important meeting brought together representatives of the world's Protestant missionary societies. The 1938 gathering was notable in that over half of the 471 participants were from the so-called "younger churches." For the first time, African Christian leaders from different parts of the continent gathered at an international conference, having traveled together by ship. Large delegations represented India and China—the two most populous homes of vigorous Asian Christian leadership. The conference called an extra session in which to hear from Jesudason and Gandhi's missionary friend Charlie Andrews about the ashram movement.[29] The next day, in plenary session, the missionary conference voted that all new foreign missionaries to India should first spend time in an ashram so as to cultivate equality with Indians and erase their biases of European superiority.[30] After the conference, a stream of sympathetic delegates from around the world traveled to Christukula. Through cross-cultural friendship, the Family of Christ had come full circle: Indian Christianity witnessed to the Western missionaries.

Twenty-Seven Years in Mao's Prisons:
Dr. Yu Enmei and the Price of Remaining

One of the saddest titles for a missionary memoir is Dorothy McCammon's *We Tried to Stay*. The title reflects how sometimes remaining is not always possible—even if people try their best to do so. Dorothy recounts how in 1947, she, her husband, Don, and three other women went to Hochwan (Hechuan), China, as Mennonite missionaries. Because the mission they entered had previously been Methodist, they planned to work with veteran Methodist missionary educators Olin and Esther Stockwell, with whom they soon became close friends. The McCammons arrived in China as the Communist armies under Mao Zedong were gradually conquering the country. Dorothy McCammon recounts how after the Communists arrived in Hochwan, they quickly transformed the landscape through indoctrination sessions, seizure of land and destruction of landlords, and show trials and mass executions.[31] She summarized the process as "the rich were now poor, the poor still poor, and the very poor a bit better off."[32]

The Mennonite missionaries, who were pacifists, lived humbly and focused on evangelism and personal relationships. They did not have a big house in a foreign compound. Nor did they own large institutions such as schools or hospitals—the particular object of Communist resentment against foreign missionaries. Thus the McCammons hoped to be allowed to stay on after the Communist takeover. This hope was in vain. The Communist regime was a vise slowly crushing them. To avoid being accused by mobs of being the "running dogs" of American imperialists, their Chinese friends started avoiding them. As long as possible, Dorothy kept relating closely to individual Chinese Christian women who were brave enough to speak with the "American imperialists." For example, she encouraged a young woman whose faith was shaken after enrolling in the Communist movement. She prayed and talked frankly with her Chinese friend "Julie," and they deepened their faith together.

The outbreak of the Korean War in 1950 pitted China against the United States in a direct way. By July 1950, therefore, the missionaries realized their presence was endangering their Chinese friends. With regret, they applied for a permit to leave China. The governing authorities dragged out the permitting process as a means of punishing the foreigners and making their lives miserable for as long as possible.

By the end of the year, Don McCammon had been arrested. On January 1, 1951, he was subject to a show trial and denunciation meeting and was condemned to death by the shouting crowd. Unknown to him, his home church in the United States was having a special prayer meeting on his behalf at the same time.[33] Olin Stockwell had already been arrested two months previously and remained in prison for two years, charged with being a spy.[34] After additional weeks of mistreatment, McCammon was deported, leaving his pregnant wife behind. For six long months, she and two other missionary women were under house confinement and constantly watched, visited, and harassed. She bore baby Julia in very difficult circumstances. Carrying her newborn, she was finally sent to a central location where Europeans were warehoused by the Chinese prior to deportation. Nine months after having last seen her husband, Dorothy McCammon and her ten-week-old baby were allowed to leave China.

Dorothy dedicated her China memoir to her two "great-hearted, God-given friends" Esther and Enmei.[35] Esther, of course, was her older missionary mentor and confidant, Esther Stockwell. With both their husbands imprisoned, they comforted each other. Although she mentions Esther by name in the book, she dared not mention Enmei except by initial, and even then, rarely.[36] For in 1951, the Communists arrested Dr. Yu Enmei.

Only after Dr. Yu was released in 1978, twenty-seven years later, did her friends learn what had happened to her. Dorothy interviewed her, and her missionary friends published her story for her ninetieth birthday in 1992. The story of Dr. Yu is a powerful testimony to friendship as remaining. As Dorothy wrote in the preface to her story, "Faithful friendship may have been the only true charge against her." And as Enmei wrote to her friends in her first letter after her release, "I never doubted . . . , even in the pitch-dark, solitary cells for nineteen months, the love and prayers of my friends."[37]

Yu Enmei was born the daughter of a poor Anglican rector in Hangzhou. In 1922, she entered on full scholarship the prestigious Ginling College for Women, one of the leading mission schools in China. Yu attended medical school, did her internship at mission hospitals, and then won a scholarship for two years of training at the Women's Medical College in Philadelphia. A postdoctoral position at Johns Hopkins School of Medicine, followed by a stint at Memorial Sloan Kettering Cancer Center in New York City, made Dr. Yu one of only two doctors in China able to use radium for treatment of cancer.

Thus it was as a highly qualified gynecologist and oncologist that Dr. Yu returned to China in 1936. During the Japanese war against China, Dr. Yu's hospital was overrun by the Japanese. She spent time in the army, trying to save the lives of wounded soldiers. By 1941, she received a missionary appointment as head of obstetrics-gynecology at the Methodist Hospital in Chongqing. During World War II, she worked under strenuous circumstances, frequently performing surgery in bomb shelters."[38] After the war ended in 1945, Dr. Yu took a badly needed furlough and sabbatical. She returned to New York for advanced work in oncology, and then returned to China in late 1947.

And then in 1949, the Communists defeated the Nationalists. In 1950, with the start of the Korean War, Americans became enemies of the state. The Communist government began expelling missionaries from China. Some were arrested and made public examples. Bishop Carleton Lacy, for example, the last Methodist bishop in China, died under house arrest. His bones were paraded through the streets. Catholic Bishop Francis Xavier Ford, a Maryknoll Father, died of torture in a Chinese prison in 1952. After the Communists arrested missionary Olin Stockwell, they put his wife under house arrest. No one was allowed to help her or buy her food, and she could not leave the hostel. Despite the danger to herself, Dr. Yu kept visiting and helping Esther Stockwell, as well as other missionaries, and bravely helped them write documents to present to the Communist government. She brought food and spent time with Mrs. Stockwell and others. None of the other Chinese Christians were brave—or foolish—enough to visit someone whose husband had been arrested as a spy. On

May 2, 1951, the Communists arrested Dr. Yu. They charged her with being an American spy, based on her relationship with the Stockwells and other missionary friends.

The story of Dr. Yu's twenty-seven years in prison is a shocking tale of starvation, torture, and abuse. It was a miracle she survived with her mind reasonably intact. At first she was put into solitary confinement and interrogated for months—no bowl for her food, nothing to lie on, no bathing, and no change of clothing. This treatment was only the beginning of years of hard labor meted out to her. Several years into her imprisonment, she tried to commit suicide. Eventually she was allowed to work in a prison clinic. During a three-year famine in the early 1960s, she tended to thousands of starving prisoners but was not allowed to say they were starving because that would have been seen as a criticism of the government. The worst period was during the Cultural Revolution from 1966 to 1976. During this period of revolutionary upheaval and destruction, there was no public practice of religion in China. Youthful Red Guards rampaged, destroyed cultural treasures, and held accusation meetings. Urban youth and supposed intellectuals were forced into hard labor in the countryside. The cult of Mao Zedong grew stronger. The influence of the Cultural Revolution was felt even in prisons. As a presumed counterrevolutionary, Dr. Yu was put into solitary confinement for nineteen months in a wet cell, from which she was not expected to emerge alive. After surviving the Cultural Revolution, she was gradually treated better. But it was another two years before she was released.

After Dr. Yu's release, she traveled to the United States to see her missionary friends again and to visit relatives who had emigrated from China. How had she survived with her sanity all those years, and also controlled her bitterness against those who abused her? During her time in prison, she was unable to reveal that she spoke English or that she was a Christian. But she sang old Anglican hymns silently to herself on a daily basis. During the Cultural Revolution, in solitary confinement, she found the words of "Lead, Kindly Light" by John Henry Newman especially meaningful:

> Lead, kindly light, amid the encircling gloom,
> lead thou me on;
> the night is dark, and I am far from home;
> lead thou me on.
> Keep thou my feet; I do not ask to see
> the distant scene; one step enough for me.

She meditated on Jesus's suffering on the cross, an unjustly condemned prisoner who forgave his tormenters. She counted the days until Christmas, and imagined herself celebrating it with her missionary friends. During Easter, she experienced God's mystical presence, with visions of forgiveness and the resurrection. As Enmei recalled to Dorothy during her interviews,

> I thought of the Christian heritage that my parents left
> me and the devotional readings, sermons and church
> services I had attended. All these memories gave me
> gifts. I always felt enriched, like a millionaire, because
> I had friends. For many days I had a vision that I would
> be released and would go to Hong Kong. Then you, Dor-

othy, came into my vision, and you and I worked on my story just like this. And I had the contents all thought out—first chapter, second chapter, and so on. That vision stayed with me for years. I thought surely I could easily have a volume or even volumes to write, and that you could be the writer. I said I wanted to write something to help other people who suffered like I suffered.[39]

Yu Enmei was strengthened in her imprisonment through Christian friendship and the memories of worship and fellowship with her missionary friends. Experiences of God's power also gave her courage. During her years as a prisoner, she had attended to many dying people. Even Communist Party members, she observed, cried out to God when they were dying, not to Mao or Marx.[40] One day in 1954, she was doing manual labor on a hilltop, and a torrential rain began. The sheets of water washed away the soil. The usual guards had taken shelter and were nowhere to be found. She was alone on the hilltop. This incident reminded her that God's power was greater than that of humans, and that guns and abuse were powerless in the face of God's might. "Through my years of suffering, I was made aware of how ridiculous, how stupid, human beings are. God is all-powerful."[41] The memory of that moment stayed with her through succeeding years of imprisonment.[42]

Chinese views of the meaning of friendship became evident when, after the Cultural Revolution, Dr. Yu's friends and relatives realized she was still alive and found her. She starting receiving letters and phone calls from the United States. The prison administration was astonished at this, and her reputation improved. Doctor Yu mused that part of her mistreatment in prison was likely because people assumed she had no friends or family. And in China, a person without friends or family is worth less than those who have them. When she was finally allowed to visit with family, her nephew made her very happy when he noticed the many friends who stepped forward to show her love: "'Auntie, I must tell you, I take my hat off to you. I think it is remarkable that you have so many friends.' It brought tears to my eyes when he went on to say, 'Do you know, one of your friends said that if you could, she would mortgage her house so that you could have the money to go to Hong Kong to be with us.'"[43]

After the end of the Cultural Revolution and Dr. Yu's release, she was finally rehabilitated and then honored for all the medical work she had done. After Dorothy McCammon interviewed her, the Stockwell family paid to publish her story. For the rest of her life, she suffered severe back pain and the aftereffects of years of imprisonment. Although missionary friends offered to take care of her, she refused. Rather, she insisted on another kind of remaining. She took her pension from the Methodist Mission Board and started a fund to educate disabled children in Chengdu. She remained in China and opened a clinic for handicapped children. Her final words in her interview with Dorothy McCammon express appreciation for prayer—a sign of the mutual friendship in Christ that characterized "God with us" in her life and those of her missionary friends: "I have so much to be thankful for in His boundless mercy and love. . . . I know that many prayers were said for me in various churches by hundreds of fellow Christians. I can testify that these sad experiences have helped me entrust my remaining life in this world to Christ, to live within me and without."[44]

Conclusion: Emmanuel and the Gift of Presence

As the stories in this chapter show, friendship as remaining is the gift of Emmanuel, "God with us." Like God's presence, faithful friendship is a matter of being. Whether seen as a spiritual discipline, an expression of kingdom hope, or a missional practice, faithful friendship embodies the presence of Jesus Christ in the lives of his followers. For Caroline Macdonald, "God as friend" was the basis for engaging Japanese prisoners and their families. And for Savarirayan Jesudason and Ernest Forrester-Paton, mutual love of Jesus and his kingdom was the spiritual bond that emboldened them to defy colonial-era racism and to launch Christukula Ashram, the "Family of Christ." Even when one is denied the physical proximity of friends in Christ, as was Dr. Yu in prison, the knowledge that they exist across social and political divisions—and are praying for you—can make the difference between life and death.

The spirituality of what is called "Christian presence" informs the idea and practice of friendship as remaining. A chief inspiration for Christian presence was the life of the French hermit Father Charles de Foucauld. At the turn of the twentieth century, he moved to the Algerian desert. He remained there as a supportive friend to all who came by—Tuareg tribespeople, French soldiers, and Arab travelers. Living alone in the desert, especially during the years of the First World War, required constant self-emptying and vulnerability.[45] Revolutionaries assassinated de Foucauld in 1916. After his death, his example and spiritual writings inspired followers to embrace Christian presence as a vulnerable spirituality of living among and serving people without coercion—or expectation of anything in return. In 1955, Father René Voillaume's inspiring reflections on the life and teachings of Charles de Foucauld were published in English. In *Seeds in the Desert*, Voillaume writes that the mission of presence is to "make Jesus' Gospel, His beatitudes and His loving friendship for the poor 'present' by living in the world."[46] Christian presence is not about "results" but about being and doing in love for Jesus and for others, especially the poor.[47] To make the kingdom of God real among people, writes Voillaume, Jesus requires "that we give ourselves in utterly disinterested friendship; that we love fraternally and tenderly all those He sends us and especially the most forsaken and those who suffer most."[48]

Just as the love of Jesus is both intimate and constant, friendship as remaining requires consistency and rootedness. As all the stories in this chapter demonstrate, it requires a long-term rather than short-term mentality and commitment to accompany each other in hope. Chris Heuertz, founder of Word Made Flesh, a network of communities of young people who live among and serve the world's poor, writes how it took him twenty years before he realized the importance of long-term commitments and "sustained friendship in community."[49] At first, when he started out, he dismissed the importance of long-term commitments to particular people and places. That kind of staying put did not fit his image of being on the spot, ready for action, in times of crisis. It was too slow, too old-fashioned and boring, for his sense of active vocation.

As Heuertz gradually discovered, the determination to remain is the precondition for embracing diverse relationships. Remaining means being present in the name of Christ. As a mustard-seed practice, faithful friendships start small and grow over time. Even so, many are strangled by the weeds of personal failures and social injustices that grow alongside them. Thus every cross-cultural relationship that grows from seed to shrub is cause for celebration. Ultimately it is God's presence that anchors friendship as remaining: the gift of Emmanuel, "God with us."

CHAPTER 4

Exile

Friendship and Family

What is an unspeakable gift of God for the
lonely individual is easily disregarded and trod-
den under foot by those who have the gift every day. It is easily forgotten that the fellowship
of Christian brethren is a gift of grace, a gift of
the Kingdom of God that any day may be taken
from us.

—Dietrich Bonhoeffer, *Life Together*

The idea of exile at first seems unrelated to friendship as
remaining. And yet, in practice, the two are interwoven. To
cross boundaries and befriend others may require leaving behind one's own home, birth family, tribe, or nation. Loyalty
to the gospel—and to the people you serve—can even make
you homeless. Jesus and his closest disciples knew this when
Jesus warned, in response to a wannabe follower, "Foxes have
holes, and birds of the air have nests; but the Son of Man has
nowhere to lay his head" (Matt. 8:20).

To remain and to experience exile are two sides of the same coin. A good illustration of the connection between remaining and exile is found in the life of China missionary Eric Liddell, the great Scottish runner. The conflict between competing for Scotland in the Olympics and his evangelical principle of keeping the Sabbath was chronicled in the movie *Chariots of Fire*. The movie narrative of Liddell's life ends with his amazing gold-medal victory in the 400 meters in the 1924 Olympics, an alternative race he selected to avoid having to compete on a Sunday.

But where the movie ended, with Liddell as a Scottish national hero, the experience of exile began. Liddell returned to China as a missionary. During the Second World War, Liddell sent his wife and three daughters to Canada while he remained serving the Chinese. In 1943, Liddell was captured and interned by the Japanese. He died in a prison camp in February 1945. Survivors remembered him as a saint. He spent time helping young people in the camp and was known for being fair and even-tempered.[1]

From the Scottish perspective, Eric Liddell died in exile. But to the Chinese, he was the first Chinese-born person to win an Olympic gold medal—a home-grown hero. Many years later, the Chinese erected a monument in his honor. Was Liddell's primary identity as a Scot or a Chinese? And to which family did he give his primary allegiance? Although Liddell loved his wife and children, by choosing to remain with the suffering Chinese people, he subsumed his individual family needs under those of the larger family of Christ. In remaining with his Chinese friends, he was exiled from the wife and children he loved. When Jesus faced the same kind of choices as Liddell, he asked the question, "'Who is my mother, and who are my brothers?' Pointing to his disciples, he said, 'Here are my mothers and my brothers. For whoever does the will of my Father in heaven is my brother and sister and mother'" (Matt. 12:48–50).

This chapter is about the entanglement of exile, family, and Christian friendship. Like Eric Liddell, the people whose stories are narrated in this chapter experienced painful exiles from people and countries they loved, for the sake of the gospel. They struggled with split loyalties to the competing sets of relationships that claimed them. And in an age of wars and revolutionary upheaval (roughly the middle third of the twentieth century), they paid a high price for embracing cross-cultural friendships.

First narrated is the surprising story of an American, Merrell Vories, and a Japanese woman, Makiko Hitotsuyanagi. Their story introduces the challenging situation of marriage between persons of enemy nations. It also brings up the important question of how marriage and Christian friendship relate to each other. The second cluster of stories examines Christians caught in the Cold War between China and the United States. Missionary-turned-ambassador John Leighton Stuart and the Philip Fugh family were exiled from Communist China; Milo and Judith Thornberry and Peng Ming-min were exiled from Taiwan. In both situations, the people involved were rejected by the countries of their birth.

These stories show that crossing cultural boundaries requires inhabiting the uneasy liminal space in which loyalty to one's ethnicity or country of birth and loyalty to one's friends in Christ are pitted against each other, involving a new level of risk and self-emptying.[2] The theme of exile reminds us that just as there is no such thing as cheap grace, there is no such thing as cheap friendship.

Friendship, Marriage, and Exile:
William Merrell Vories and Makiko Hitotsuyanagi

In 1905, the twenty-four-year-old Merrell Vories from Colorado College got off the train in Omi Province, Japan. He did not know a soul, nor did he speak Japanese. When he died in 1964, he was a Japanese citizen named Mereru Hitotsuyanagi. With a Japanese team, he had designed over 1,500 buildings in Japan and Korea, including YMCA buildings, churches, schools, residences, and commercial buildings.[3] He and his associates ran a comprehensive mission that transformed life for many in Omi. His wife, Makiko Hitotsuyanagi Vories, was a highly educated woman from the Japanese imperial family. When they married in 1919, she lost her Japanese citizenship but was denied the right to become an American citizen. The story of their lives is a tale of how their commitment to the family of Christ, and to embodying the kingdom of God, came before national loyalties. It is also a story of how friendship and marriage united for common goals.

Merrell Vories was a member of the Student Volunteer Movement for Foreign Missions. He felt called by God to be a pioneer, self-supporting missionary somewhere where there was no Christian presence. He left his studies in architecture and went by steamer and train to the Buddhist enclave of Omi-Hachiman, Japan, to teach English in a commercial high school. Consumed with homesickness, he prayed to God for a Christian friend. Unknown to him, a Japanese Christian named B. C. Miyamoto had been praying for two years that God would send another Christian to Omi. Their finding each other was an answer to both men's prayers.[4] Miyamoto visited Vories and asked him to lead a Bible study. He even interpreted for him from English to Japanese.[5] As a freelance missionary with neither foreign infrastructure nor a family to consider, Vories plunged into Japanese life. He quickly bonded with teenage boys who, out of curiosity to see the foreigner, flocked to his home for recreation and Bible study. Vories and his pupils rapidly became friends. Numerous youths moved in with him to create a kind of settlement house they called "the family." Vories recalled, "My response to the friendliness of these new friends, my pupils, must have been as transparently evident as it was genuine, for immediately there began a spontaneous cordiality between us—which was radically different from the conventional Oriental relations between teacher and pupils."[6] Reflecting on the radical cultural immersion he experienced, Vories wrote, "The succeeding days of quick, yet deep and enduring, fellowships taught me the superficiality of racial and national distinctions, in the face of human sympathy and brotherhood. From that time onward not only was race-prejudice eliminated from my experience, but even race-consciousness."[7] Within three years, Vories had attracted such a large following of pupils to Christ, roughly 40 percent of the school, that he was fired from his job as English teacher.

For the ministry to survive without his income from teaching, Vories and a few companions lived in common and ate only rice. He returned to his profession of architecture in order to fund the mission. In 1908, he opened an architectural office that quickly found clients for YMCA, church, and educational enterprises that wished to adapt simple but modern Western forms to Japanese lifestyles and artistry. For the next thirty-five years, Vories employed dozens of new Christians as managers and draftsmen for hundreds of projects. Even though he kept costs low and refused to give or receive bribes, profits from architecture paid for the expanding mission. In addition, Vories obtained the Japanese rights to a menthol ointment called Mentholatum. The manufacture and distribution of Mentholatum, popularly known as "Jesus salve," also funded outreach.

In 1934, Vories and his Japanese associates renamed the Omi Mission the Omi Brotherhood to reflect the deeper meaning of their fellowship as one of Jesus's way of mutuality under God rather than of missionary paternalism.[8] As a witness to Christian values in Japanese industry, the brotherhood insisted on Sabbath rest and an eight-hour workday for construction workers, no bribery, no alcohol or tobacco, and no price gouging. The brotherhood also shared employee ownership, and employees received stipends rather than salaries. Profits were invested in ministry.[9] Over the years, the Omi Brotherhood transformed Omi through ministry projects, including a tuberculosis sanatorium, youth centers, farming cooperatives, Christian publications, churches, and schools. Former students of Vories's took key roles as team leaders and managers of the different departments of the Omi Brotherhood, including finance. An executive committee of fifteen— including Vories, his Japanese cofounders, and elected representatives of the departments—operated by consensus in monthly, daylong meetings. All property belonged to "members in common."[10]

The communitarianism of Vories and his Japanese partners reflected an amalgamation of disciplined samurai ethics with Christian egalitarianism and American entrepreneurial spirit. It also represented Vories's firm ideals that only through international relationships could the kingdom of God be built. To counteract the problem of superpatriotism sweeping over the world after World War I, Vories believed the parable of the good Samaritan needed to apply to international life—that the "neighbor" had to include people from nations and cultures other than one's own. Therefore, the leadership team of the Omi Brotherhood included "at least the four Nationalities which are most closely thrown together politically and industrially in the Pacific basin—Japanese, Americans, Chinese, and Koreans. If in a small organization like ours these four may not achieve equality and brotherhood, then we might as well give up any fond dreams of harmony on a larger scale."[11] As relations grew worse among the different countries, the Omi Brotherhood became even more intentional in showing that men from all four nations could cooperate in the name of Christ.

Having embraced Japanese culture, and even having brought his parents to live with him in Japan, Vories sought unity across cultural boundaries—notably through music. Vories and his Japanese musician friends shared a mutual love of Western classical and church music. This dynamic can be seen in Vories's intimate bonding with Japanese violinist Goro Takagi, a self-taught prodigy. According to Vories's biography of his friend, they met in 1926 when Takagi was playing in a ship's orchestra, and immediately Vories began accompanying Takagi on piano. An accomplished pianist and hymn writer, Vories had become a church organist at age fourteen. For the rest of his life, at every possible moment, including on shipboard, he played the organ.[12] Takagi was impressed with Vories's ethical Christian witness, and he caught a vision of using music to serve society. He became a Christian, mastered business skills, and moved to Omi to become Vories's private secretary.[13] For him, as in the parable of the good Samaritan, "being a Christian meant brotherhood."[14] In Omi, Takagi and Vories experimented with a worship series called "Worship in Music," which combined silent scriptural meditation with "continuous sacred music" played by organ and violin.[15] Vories's account of their private evenings spent playing Western classical music together, always ending on hymns and silent prayer, described perfect spiritual unanimity: "There was absolutely no consciousness of nationality, race, age difference, or other physical limitation. For the moment we dwelt in the realm of the spirit, and became almost literally 'Two souls with but a single thought, Two hearts that beat as one.'"[16] For Takagi, being a musician was a holy calling, a "priesthood" through which the voice of God could be heard. Takagi wrote that music could create "harmony in our social world."[17] Despite their difference in age and nationality, their friendship, wrote Vories, showed them the "possibilities of Love."[18] They believed music was a universal language given by God. The friendship between Goro Takagi and Merrell Vories illustrates how music has been and remains one of the most important means by which Christians in different cultures can find each other.

Merrell Vories's most daring cross-cultural friendship resulted in his marriage in 1919, at age thirty-nine, to thirty-five-year-old Makiko Hitotsuyanagi. Theirs was a friendship of equals, as they were bound together in a "third space" of Christian fellowship that transcended both Japanese and American cultures. Maki was from a noble Japanese family. She was unusual in refusing to marry the suitors selected by her family. Instead, at age twenty-four, she went to the United States to study. She remained there for nine years, where she was baptized in a Presbyterian church. She supported herself by working as a live-in companion for an elderly woman until her family demanded her return to Japan. She and Merrell met when Merrell came to her brother's house to discuss designs for a house and commercial buildings, and her brother asked her to sit in on the discussions. By the time they met, each was at home in the other's culture. Both were musicians, she a pianist and he an organist. Both had a strong commitment to transforming society toward care for the poor and disabled, gender and racial equality, and the eradication of class differences.

Both their families strenuously opposed the marriage for racial and national reasons. An additional problem was that Maki was from the imperial household and Merrell was a penniless commoner, and no aristocratic women were allowed to marry commoners. In order to marry Merrell across class, national, and ethnic lines, Maki renounced her place in the imperial family. Their wedding took place in a church, with the bride in a white gown, before crisscrossed Japanese and American flags. Over many decades of happy marriage, Maki shared in the communal life her husband had developed.

She moved right into the poor neighborhood where he lived, rolled up her sleeves, and got to work. She expanded the work of the Omi Brotherhood into outreach for women and girls, most notably through the founding of kindergartens and other children's educational initiatives. She also began educating and helping the Burakumin, then known as Eta, or "filth," an outcast group of miserably poor people considered the untouchables of Japanese society.

Despite Merrell and Maki's happy partnership, the deteriorating political situation between Japan and the United States undermined their legal status. Upon renouncing her nobility, Maki effectively lost her Japanese citizenship, for in Japan, it was legally impossible to be a citizen without a place in a Japanese family. When they married, the American consul had welcomed Maki. But by 1925, when she tried to get a passport to travel to the United States, the Oriental Exclusion Act of 1924 forbade even the Japanese wives of Americans from becoming citizens. Maki discovered that she was now a woman without a country—despite having an American husband and having previously lived in the United States for many years. Her shock and anger were followed by resignation born of her Christian faith. As she contemplated the meaning of her exile in theological terms, Maki decided that perhaps being liberated from nationalism was a good thing: "I was now, purely and simply, a citizen only of the Kingdom of God, free from any human concern. This gave me a real sense of freedom."[19]

As World War II approached, Merrell faced a stark choice. The Japanese military invaded China and Korea. Emperor veneration was required of everyone. Christian schools were being closed, and missionaries were leaving. Hostility to foreigners, such as himself, was increasing. He felt that in case of war, the Japanese would suffer badly and then lose. And he loved the United States. But Merrell also had chosen to live with and for the Japanese people. In the past he had been critical of foreigners who moved to the United States and enjoyed its benefits but who failed to take on the responsibilities of citizenship. Was he a hypocrite in not becoming a Japanese citizen? And what about Maki, who was a woman without a country? So in 1940, Merrell applied for Japanese nationality. He decided that his Christian witness required suffering with his adopted people. Caught between countries, he hoped that by becoming a Japanese citizen during a time of war, he could more easily bridge East and West. Neither side had the whole truth. As he wrote in a poem,

> For the West alone and the East alone
> In their half-truths grope and fall;
> Yet we wait the day when with hearts as one
> We shall brothers be through the Holy Son,
> The Father of us all.[20]

The process of becoming a Japanese citizen was difficult for more than one reason. This process entailed Maki divorcing Merrell to reestablish her Japanese citizenship and then quickly remarrying him, though as a commoner. She then turned over family leadership to Merrell, who was required to adopt her family name of Hitotsuyanagi. Now as Mereru Hitotsuyanagi, at age sixty-one, Merrell underwent a Shinto shrine ceremony, pledged his allegiance to the emperor, and took his place in Hitotsuyanagi ancestral rituals. The focus of Shinto on venerating the ancestors was valued by Merrell, and he had already erected a mausoleum to preserve and honor his parents' ashes with regular prayers. But as a Christian, how could he defend theologically a decision that put him on the side of what many Christians considered to be idolatry?

In a thoughtful defense of his controversial decision, Merrell Vories rejected the idea that State Shinto was religious. He believed emperor veneration was a civil act rather like saying the Pledge of Allegiance. The Shinto priest who performed the citizenship ceremony recognized that Merrell was a Christian. In a deeper theological justification based on what is now called "inculturation," Merrell argued that the incarnation of Jesus into humanity was itself a form of "naturalization." Thus the giving of himself to the Japanese people was a sign of his love for Japan and for his wife. In following the example of Jesus, he wrote, "At least I can share in the sufferings of those I love and the land of my adoption."[21] The best way that he could show love for the Japanese, for fellow workers, and for his "life-companion" was by becoming Japanese during their time of trial. To Merrell, "faithful friendship" confirmed his witness as a Christian, even if it meant crossing boundaries of religion and nation.

One of the important issues raised by the example of Merrell and Maki is the connection between marriage and friendship. In classical writings about friendship, the possibility of friendship between man and woman is rejected. If friendship must be between equals, and ancient society considered women to be lower than men, then friendship with women was not possible. Sexual tension between men and women made friendships with women unlikely. Later philosophers of Christian friendship also faced the problem that Jesus's words seemed to pit the friendship of the disciples against loyalty to family. Thus if one was practicing the faith, the higher loyalty needed to be to the family of Christ, not one's biological family. Protestant cleric Jeremy Taylor broke with the typical position that Christian friendship and marriage were separate. In fact, he argued that Christian marriage "is the Queen of friendships, in which there is a communication of all that can be communicated by friendship: and . . . made sacred by vowes and love, by bodies and souls, by interest and custome, by religion and by lawes."[22] A good marriage could embody friendship, with two people intimately entwined and supported by the sanctity of law.

Merrell and Maki would have agreed with Taylor. To them, Christian fellowship, marriage, and their personal friendship were one of a piece. Merrell took Taylor's argument a step further by suggesting that interracial marriage is the ultimate ideal in the kingdom of God. Marriage between persons from different countries brings together different cultures in ways that benefit the total "progress" of humanity. Merrell acknowledged that celibacy was good for the sake of the ministry. But the right marriage, in which the partners together followed the "Plan of God," actually increased missionary effectiveness. "It is not marriage, but a wrong marriage, that does the damage," he wrote.[23] Married as two mature adults committed to Christian principles, Merrell and Maki embodied the ideal of cross-cultural marriage as faithful friendship. In so doing, their view of family rested in the fellowship of Christ. Thus when push came to shove, they chose to stand with each other and with the ideals of the kingdom of God and to reject knee-jerk, patriotic nationalism.

After the bombing of Pearl Harbor, the realities of exile grew more intense for the couple. Despite technically becoming Japanese, Merrell faced prejudice and hostility. In this, he shared similar experiences with other expat spouses who lived in Japan during World War II, most of whom were women. There are several very moving accounts of American Christian women, married to Japanese, who lived in Japan during the war. With gender inequality embedded in both American and Japanese tradition, foreign women who married Japanese were considered Japanese, as they became part of their husbands' family lineage. In the United States, after the bombing of Pearl Harbor, American women married to Japanese were interned along with their husbands and deported to Japan. American-born Gwen Terasaki, for example, nearly starved to death while her husband tried to seclude her and their mixed-race daughter from the Japanese military in fear of what would happen to them.[24] Alice Kurusu was married to Ambassador Saburō Kurusu, who famously was trying to negotiate with the United States at the time Japan bombed Pearl Harbor.[25] They were interned and deported to Japan. Although their daughters eventually married Americans and returned to the United States, their son Ryō was killed while serving in the Japanese military during the war and is the only Eurasian buried at Japan's famous war memorial, the Yasukuni Shrine. If Merrell and Maki had gone to the United States, things would not have been any better. No doubt Maki would have been arrested if they had tried to weather the war in the United States.

During the war, the Vories-Hitotsuyanagis were assumed to be American spies and were treated with great suspicion, even by people who had known them for years. They tried to avoid leaving their home. The military confiscated their hospital and seized most of the Mentholatum they produced. A friendly visit by the younger brother of the emperor saved them from worse treatment by townspeople and paramilitary forces. Because of the hostility they faced, they exiled themselves to the countryside for the bulk of the war. Merrell suffered a heart attack. Maki grew extremely ill from starvation and nearly died of typhus. Merrell's bedridden, incontinent mother was also with them, miserable at being separated from her other children in the United States. The ongoing hunger and stress caused severe depression.

Relief came only after the war ended. Despite broken health and destroyed facilities, Merrell and Maki did what they could to promote peace and reconciliation between the Japanese and the American people. They raised funds in the United States and rebuilt what they could of the Omi Brotherhood and continued their work—this time as honored citizens. Then Merrell had severe strokes. For the last seven years of his life, he was paralyzed, mute, and bedridden. His devoted wife took care of him, just as she had cared for his parents until their deaths. She continued her educational work running schools in Omi. When Merrell died in 1964, they had been married for forty-five years—lovers, partners, faithful friends in Christ to the end.

Out in the Cold (War):
John Leighton Stuart and the Philip Fugh Family;
Milo and Judith Thornberry and Peng Ming-min

"A revolution is not a dinner party, or writing an essay, or painting a picture, or doing embroidery; it cannot be so refined, so leisurely and gentle, so temperate, kind, courteous, restrained and magnanimous. A revolution is an insurrection, an act of violence by which one class overthrows another."[26] This quotation by Mao Zedong encapsulates the challenges for cross-cultural friendship in the mid-twentieth century during the period called the Cold War. Exile from one's friends, and exile for the sake of one's friends, became common. Friendship as exile meant being caught between rather than being fully at home in one place. It could be physical—being forced to leave places and peoples one loves. It could also be psychological—a sense of alienation felt while living in one's own country, separated from loved ones who have been demonized by political divides.

At the time of the Communist victory in 1948, there were an estimated four million Christians in China, only a small percentage of the population. Most Chinese viewed Christianity as a foreign religion. With the outbreak of the Korean War in 1950, both missionaries and Chinese Christians were condemned as imperialists. As we saw in the last chapter with the story of Dr. Yu Enmei and the Mennonite missionaries, Chinese Christians had to ask specifically that their Western friends not contact them anymore. Association with Westerners became dangerous. All foreign missionaries were expelled or arrested in China. Four hundred thousand Chinese signed the "Christian Manifesto" that condemned the church as an imperialist entity. During the Cultural Revolution (1966–76), the Christian vision of "one body under heaven" was challenged by continuous class struggle, with religious people as targets. All churches were closed, public worship ended, and Christian leaders, forced to publicly confess their supposed imperialist leanings, were sent to labor camps and prisons.

In 1949, the defeated Nationalist government, and an estimated two million people, fled to the island of Taiwan. Many Christians were among them, including the leader Chiang Kai-shek. But life in Taiwan was no bed of roses. The ever-looming fear of mainland China meant that the Nationalists ruled with an iron hand. This scenario of "two Chinas" was a major diplomatic problem for the United States. President Harry S. Truman withheld support of Communist China. Instead, he recognized the defeated Nationalist regime in Taiwan as the true China. Mao was furious at the United States, which did not recognize the Chinese Communist government until 1979.

The Cold War between the West and the Communist superpowers of China and Russia triggered military buildups, proxy wars, and fear worldwide. This period of history was especially challenging for cross-cultural friendships among Christians. In the cauldron of Cold War politics, yesterday's friend was today's collaborator. People who had been lauded as bridge figures between East and West were newly judged as sellouts and assimilationist traitors. And anyone associated with a missionary was immediately suspected of being a capitalistic, Cold War "warrior."

Christian friendship as exile is illustrated by the odyssey of John Leighton Stuart, a fourth-generation Presbyterian minister born in China of missionary parents.[27] Stuart was from an old Southern family with close relationships to that of President Woodrow Wilson. He was sent to the United States for his college and seminary education, and he returned to China as a New Testament scholar. Stuart recognized that "the best security in China lies in personal relationships"[28] and that Chinese "civilization, moral philosophy and ethical standards are founded on human relationships."[29] Becoming the first president of Yenching University in 1919, he designed the campus in Chinese style in hopes of reducing its foreign ambiance. His visionary leadership made Yenching, now the campus of Peking (Beijing) University, one of the top universities in China. He was famous for treating Chinese staff as equals.[30] Unlike most mission institutions of the day, Yenching workers of all nationalities lived side by side in identical houses. After Stuart's wife of twenty-two years died in 1926, he never remarried, which only increased his closeness to the Chinese people among whom he lived. In effect, with the loss of his wife, other Chinese Christians became his extended family.

Stuart's deep capacity for friendship with Chinese colleagues can be seen in his correspondence with T. T. Liu, one of his closest associates at Yenching University. Liu studied both psychology and theology in the United States, earning his doctorate, and in 1921, he became dean of the Theology School at Yenching. He has been remembered as an innovative liturgical scholar who indigenized liturgies and hymns in Chinese, a prolific writer, and one who laid foundations for Christian education.[31] As someone who easily moved back and forth between America and China, he played important bridging roles between church leaders in both countries, especially during the Second World War.[32]

Correspondence between Liu and Stuart, when Liu was residing in the United States and Stuart was in China during the 1930s, reveals deep affection and Christian friendship. In letters, they addressed each other as "My dear Leighton" or even "My very much loved Timothy." Topics of correspondence included Liu's family, his financial situation, the controversy over his teaching career in America, the problem of "brain drain," and future planning for Yenching. Stuart expressed consistent friendship and affection for Liu even as Liu struggled with ambitions that put him at odds with other Chinese colleagues at Yenching. Some of the most poignant correspondence occurred in the last few months of Liu's life as he struggled with the disease that killed him. Stuart wrote in May 1947, just two months before Liu died, "I love you as I always have these many years of our friendship and you have more than lived up to my earliest hopes for you."[33] Liu's appreciation for his friend Stuart was expressed not only in correspondence but indirectly in a speech he gave in the late 1930s titled "Post-War Planning and the Chinese Church: A Preliminary Study of Some of the Essential Features." In this paper, Liu lists the contributions of missionaries to China. The first, naturally, is the introduction of Jesus Christ to the Chinese. But the second contribution Liu lists is "the friendships formed between them and the Chinese; and the friendship they helped form among the Chinese themselves."[34] That Liu put friendship second on the list, even before founding churches, shows how deeply he appreciated the personal relationships between Chinese Christian leaders and missionaries. Friendships persisted, despite the ongoing criticisms of missionary paternalism that leaders like Liu spearheaded.

In 1938, the Japanese invaded Beijing. Stuart refused to submit to their orders and continued to defy them in numerous ways. After the attack on Pearl Harbor, the Japanese imprisoned him for nearly four years. He was already in his sixties, though unlike Eric Liddell, Stuart survived the war.

Despite Stuart's lifetime of solidarity with the Chinese people, the rising tide of Cold War politics discredited him. At age seventy, he was appointed US ambassador. At that point in time, 1946, he was one of the most respected, most experienced experts on China in the world. Stuart recommended negotiating with the Communists, who were steadily gaining ground in their fight against the Nationalists. But he was recalled from China by the US government in 1949 in the midst of increasing fear of Communism and worsening relationships. His policy of "constructive engagement" was condemned as selling out the Nationalists. Ironically, Mao Zedong condemned him as the symbol of Western imperialism, writing in the article "Farewell, Leighton Stuart" that Stuart "was always a loyal agent of U.S. cultural aggression in China."[35] John Leighton Stuart, therefore, became Mao's whipping boy for American imperialism in China, while in the United States he was blamed for appeasement of the Communists and the "loss" of China. The US would not appoint another ambassador to the newly formed People's Republic of China until thirty years after Stuart's departure.

Returning to the United States, Stuart was accompanied by the family of his assistant and close friend, Philip Fugh. Stuart was never allowed to return to China in his lifetime, despite the fact that he was born there, his parents and brother and wife were buried there, and he had spent his life serving the Chinese people and suffering with them during the Second World War. Stuart and the Fughs lived together for thirteen years, and the Fughs cared for him for years before he died. John Fugh, Philip's son, recalled that it was very unusual for a US ambassador to have a Chinese assistant, and that Stuart had to defend his choice. Years later, John Fugh was asked whether his father was on the side of the Communists or the Nationalists, and he replied, "Neither. He worked for Ambassador Stuart."[36] The friendship between Stuart and the Fugh family made them both suspect in their home countries.

Lifelong friendship turned into exile for both the Fugh and Stuart families. Upon his death in 1962, Stuart wished to be buried in China next to his wife. But because he was the personal target of Mao, Stuart's wishes were denied. Until his death in 1988, Philip Fugh tried unsuccessfully to rebury Stuart in China. The Stuart-Fugh family relationship continued into another generation. Fugh's son, John, was the first Chinese American military general. Forty-six years after Stuart's death, in 2008, General Fugh was able to negotiate the burial of his adopted grandfather, John Leighton Stuart, next to Stuart's parents in Hangzhou.[37] US Ambassador J. Stapleton Roy, who had also grown up in China as a Presbyterian missionary kid, said Stuart's reburial "represents the finest traditions of both the United States and China, in terms of duty and loyalty, passing on an uncompleted task from one generation to the next, and ensuring that it is finally carried out successfully under adverse conditions."[38] Ambassador Roy's own father, leading missionary educator Andrew Tod Roy, had himself refused to leave China when the Communists took over and was therefore put under house arrest, then imprisoned and subjected to a show trial. He and his wife were expelled from China in 1951.[39]

The shifting meaning of John Leighton Stuart's relationships with the Chinese people shows the complexities of cross-cultural friendship in light of the binaries and polarizations of Cold War politics. Communist anti-imperialism meant that despite his lifetime of loyalty to the Chinese, Stuart became persona non grata in China. He had been born in China, and when forced out, he had to leave the graves of his parents, brother, and wife there. Yet his close personal relationship with the Fugh family was such that they moved to the United States with him and took care of him for the rest of his life. Their faithful friendship resulted in the creation of a new extended family that experienced exile together. Ironically, only after the political situation shifted past the divisions of the Cold War could the relationship between Stuart and the Chinese people be acknowledged with his reburial in China. John Leighton Stuart and the Fugh family came out of the cold when the changing political situation allowed for John Fugh to fulfill his promise to his own father, Philip, that he would arrange for Stuart to be buried in China.

Stuart's reburial in China illustrates how faithful friendship enlarges the meaning of family to an inclusive vision of the multiethnic family of Christ, joined together in life, death, and life beyond death. To be buried "in exile" may actually represent the ultimate act of "remaining." The ceremony to rebury Stuart's ashes was attended by both Chinese and American officials. The gravestone has his name in both Chinese and English. The final act of the reburial was when elderly former students from the former Yenching University put flowers on his grave and bowed three times to their teacher. The long exile had ended, and Stuart was home.

John Leighton Stuart's story ends well. But in the political climate of the Cold War, some of the most challenging situations occurred in cross-cultural friendships between Americans and those threatened by allies of the US government. During the 1960s and 1970s, the United States propped up repressive regimes around the world because they claimed to be fighting Communism. Thus, to oppose the Filipino dictator Ferdinand Marcos or the fascist Chilean strongman General Augusto Pinochet or the murderous regime of Korean president Park Chung-hee was also to oppose the official position of the United States. After missionaries were thrown out of China around 1950, many went to Hong Kong. Others went to Taiwan.

A brief reference to the story of American Methodists Milo and Judith Thornberry adds another twist to the complicated picture of faithful friendships during the Cold War. They went to Taiwan as missionaries in 1967. As they entered into the life of the people, the Thornberrys became close friends with pro-democracy activist Peng Ming-min, from a strong Presbyterian pastor's family.[40] They learned that the Taiwanese government, propped up by the United States because of its opposition to Communism, became an increasingly oppressive military dictatorship that arrested and killed democracy activists in the name of anti-Communism. Peng was a specialist in international law who had become suspicious of his own government when it wanted him to spy on Taiwanese independence groups. The Thornberrys and Peng met on a weekly basis for four years. Milo Thornberry smuggled information out of the country about the realities in Taiwan, supported the families of those arrested, and became an informant for Amnesty International to publicize the names of the thousands being secretly arrested. In 1970, the Thornberrys doctored a passport, arranged a disguise, and smuggled Peng out of the country to Sweden. Because of their friendships with pro-democracy church leaders, they were expelled from Taiwan, even though nobody realized at the time they had smuggled out Peng. Because Taiwan was a partner of the United States, Milo Thornberry was essentially persecuted for his political views by the US government and denied a renewal of his passport.

For the Thornberrys, being a friend meant not only being expelled from Taiwan but also being treated as traitors by their own government. With Richard Nixon as president and the Vietnam War in full force, friendships between Americans and those perceived as Cold War enemies were considered treasonous acts. Yet the Thornberrys put their friendship with Peng above their own safety and kept the secret for many decades of how they helped smuggle him out of Taiwan. Loyalty to Peng resulted not only in external exile from Taiwan but also internal exile within the United States itself.

The experiences of Milo and Judith Thornberry underscore how shifting political alliances can affect the course of cross-cultural friendship. Their relationship with Peng Ming-min also shows how friendships have changed the course of history. When Taiwan held its first free elections in 1996, Peng

Ming-min came out of two decades in exile to run for president as a member of a major opposition party.

Conclusion: Fellowship, Family, and Life Together

The stories in this chapter continue the theme of exile that begins in the Bible and extends through history. The Hebrew Bible places profound emphasis on the exilic experiences of the Jewish people. Their forty years spent wandering in the desert shaped the Habiru, the wandering and outcast strangers, into a community that has existed for thousands of years. In his teachings and religious practices, Jesus drew upon this biblical tradition of exile.

For followers of Jesus down through the ages, however, being a pilgrim people is not about creating a nation in the ethnic sense. Rather, the notion of exile feeds the definition of Christian community as a multicultural fellowship that exists across time and space. This fellowship is a new universal family composed of people related to Christ. It transcends ethnicity or nation. It foreshadows shalom, the state of peace and unity that will one day constitute the reign of God.

Christian fellowship and exile together mold kingdom community. This insight was precious to Dietrich Bonhoeffer, the Protestant theologian martyred in 1945 for plotting to assassinate Adolf Hitler. Hitler had tried to force the Protestant churches of Germany into supporting anti-Semitic and pro-government policies. His attempt to create a false family of Christian ethnic nationalists provoked the formation of a new family: resisters to Hitler's policies. This group called itself the

"Confessing Church." By 1937, with the arrest of hundreds of its pastors, it was increasingly forced underground. It went into exile within its own country. The head of the Nazi secret police, Heinrich Himmler, declared illegal the training of Confessing Church candidates for ministry. Bonhoeffer kept teaching the seminarians on the run, as they dodged arrest. Christian leaders who opposed the Nazis were forcibly cut off from the world church and even isolated from each other. And so they cherished Christian fellowship as a precious gift.

In his book *Life Together*, Bonhoeffer writes how believers were a "scattered seed," dispersed in exile around the world. Given this reality, the physical presence of other believers was an incredible blessing—an act of God's grace. In his loneliness, the constant awareness of the existence of Christian community gave him the strength to keep going. Even though he could not always see it physically or feel it emotionally, for Bonhoeffer, the living Christian community was a "divine reality" that extended from this life to the next. In words that seem prophetic of his own later arrest by the Nazis, he wrote,

> What is an unspeakable gift of God for the lonely individual is easily disregarded and trodden under foot by those who have the gift every day. It is easily forgotten that the fellowship of Christian brethren is a gift of grace, a gift of the Kingdom of God that any day may be taken from us. . . . Therefore, let him who until now has had the privilege of living a common Christian life with other Christians praise God's grace from the bottom of his heart. Let him thank God on his knees and declare:

It is grace, nothing but grace, that we are allowed to live
in community with fellow Christians.[41]

Prayers, letters, common worship, retreats with other Christians—all these express community with each other in Jesus
Christ.[42]

With Jesus Christ as "our Brother," Bonhoeffer continues,
Christians begin to understand the meaning of love toward
one another. "I am a brother to another person through
what Jesus Christ did for me and to me; the other person
has become a brother to me through what Jesus Christ did
for him. . . . What determines our brotherhood is what that
man is by reason of Christ. Our community with one another
consists solely in what Christ has done to both of us."[43] Ultimately, Christian community is neither an ideal nor a matter
of emotion but a gift from God.

In his writings, Bonhoeffer implies that particular friendships cannot be equated with the divine gift of Christian fellowship. But I would argue that his connection of exile with
the formation of the wider family of Christ resonates with
faithful friendship as a biblical and historical practice. As
the examples in this book show, cross-cultural friendships
can embody the new family of Christ at the heart of wider
Christian fellowship. Through shared exile across national
and ethnic differences, William Merrell Vories and Makiko
Hitotsuyanagi created a new family that witnessed to unity
in Christ. John Leighton Stewart and Philip Fugh, and the
Thornberrys with Peng Ming-min, showed how the shared
Christian family resisted the oppressive political conditions
that tried to divide it.

The hard lesson of exile teaches that Christian fellowship can transcend challenging political and social differences. While moments of transcendence may be difficult, and witness against hypernationalistic ethnocentrism too rare, the stories in this chapter show that they nevertheless exist. Such moments demonstrate that faithful friendship is not cheap or easy. Faithful friendships may not be equated with the fullness of Christian fellowship, in all its ecclesiological and contextual complexity, but they seed it from the bottom up. Like the mustard seed, cross-cultural Christian friendships start small. Yet, amid exile, the new family of Christ grows deep roots. It keeps kingdom hopes alive.

CHAPTER 5

Testimony

Friendship and Struggle

> Racial reconciliation is whites and blacks hold-
> ing on to each other, not letting go, and doing
> surgery on each other.
>
> —Tom Skinner

Friendship is a struggle.

External struggle can make friendship nearly impossible. When political, social, and ethnic divisions run high,
friends must cross a lot of boundaries to stay in communion with each other. When lines are being drawn in the
sand, the friend is called to step across to embrace the
person on the other side—but faces ridicule or worse for
doing so.

And second, friendship can be an internal struggle. The
personal misunderstandings, feelings of uncertainty or even
betrayal, the sense of being ignored . . . friendships are made,
and friendships are broken. It is not surprising that the external and internal struggles often feed each other.

At their best, the struggles of friendship testify to God's grace. As friends grapple together, they cocreate a new narrative of grace. They anchor a reality that is greater than their natural divisions and human disappointments. Through struggle, their relationship becomes a transcendent testimony of love and reconciliation that points to the kingdom of God. Whether they fail or succeed in changing the world is not the point. At the very least, by embracing diversity they have themselves been changed in relationship with the "other."

The stories in this chapter are about friendships in times of struggle, and friendships as struggle. Both kinds of struggle have produced powerful testimonies to the values of unity, justice, and reconciliation. The first takes place during the Rhodesian civil war of 1965–79 and reveals the interracial friendship of white Afrikaner Inus Daneel and black Shona bishop Matteo Forridge. Along with other leaders in their theological training program, they shared the common goals of ecumenical unity and the empowerment of poor churches. Their friendship testified that commitment to Christian unity could transcend racial and cultural differences, even in wartime.

The second story examines how friendship gave believers courage for the struggle—the strength to cross cultural boundaries and to confront political injustice on behalf of the oppressed. The friends were American missionaries and the American wives of Korean theologians who met weekly for spiritual support in Korea during the early 1970s. The "Monday night group" prepared its participants for personal and family upheaval in the face of social trauma. These participants' testimonies of friendship extended outward to challenge shocking human rights abuses under the dictatorship of President Park.

The final story examines the interracial friendship between Spencer Perkins and Chris Rice as they testified to racial reconciliation in Mississippi during the 1980s. Their story is unusual because it carefully documents the inner struggles of friendship embedded in the external struggle of race relations between blacks and whites in the Deep South. Their candid sharing of their pilgrimage of friendship gives hope in the context of entrenched racism.

Inus Daneel and Matteo Forridge:
Church Unity and Interracial Solidarity

On November 11, 1965, missionary M. L. "Inus" Daneel was helping deliver a baby in the back of his Land Cruiser in rural Rhodesia. The Shona woman was having a difficult delivery, and Daneel was taking her from her small village to the mission hospital. But the baby wouldn't wait. With no running water, his hands were covered with blood as he assisted the midwife with the delivery. He switched on the car radio. On came the prime minister of Rhodesia. Daneel heard Ian Smith declare independence from Great Britain and announce the "self-government" of Rhodesia—the rule of 220,000 whites over four million blacks. Smith framed his declaration in terms of the Cold War, as a blow against Communism in the "Afro-Asian block." He announced to the world, "We have struck a blow for the preservation of justice, civilization, and Christianity; and in the spirit of this belief we have this day assumed our sovereign independence. God bless you all."[1]

With the blood of life on his hands, Daneel's heart sank when he heard Smith on the radio, for he knew that the blood of many violent deaths would follow. And so it did. After the UDI, the "unilateral declaration of independence," came fifteen years of brutal civil war defined largely by race. The liberation war pitted blacks against whites and Africans of one tribe or political persuasion against others. The war ended in 1979 when South Africa finally withdrew its support from white Rhodesia. In 1980, the black majority–ruled country Zimbabwe was born.

To be friends with someone from another race during a racial civil war was to court death. Churches were divided by race. As the child of missionary parents, Inus Daneel had grown up on a mission station that sponsored over six hundred schools in rural areas. Missionaries rejoiced when the Shona people joined the Reformed church. But to white farmers, black people were useful primarily as farm laborers and servants. Being fellow Christians did not translate into worshipping together on Sundays.

Missionaries working in rural areas were caught between Rhodesian and opposition forces. Two of Inus Daneel's close friends in the Dutch Reformed Church, the Reverend Andre Brand and his wife, Bieneke, were attacked by guerilla fighters when they were returning home from administering Communion in the rural areas. The fighters shot Rev. Brand with AK-47s. Mrs. Brand tried to run away but tripped and hit her head on a stone. According to the eyewitness account of the Shona pastor who was with the Brands but managed to escape, a guerilla fighter walked up to Mrs. Brand and calmly shot her in the head. Their deaths left six children with no parents.

Because of racism in the white churches, as well as a desire to have their own leaders and worship in ways that were culturally meaningful, a lot of black Christians had already founded what were called African Independent Churches (AICs).[2] During the colonial period of the early to mid-twentieth century, African Christian leaders across the continent broke away from mission churches and founded their own. With their focus on healing, visions, the exorcism of evil spirits, polygamy, and reliance on strong leaders, AICs put the gospel into terms meaningful to Africans.[3] A few visionary, nontraditional missionaries opened doors to relationships with AICs on the basis of equality rather than with the aim of trying to convert them back to Western churches. Summarizing the struggle of friendship between Western missionaries and AICs, Mennonite theologian David A. Shank writes, "The long-term building of relationships of trust, openness and true reciprocity in Christ may be the hardest but most effective 'Good News' that an expatriate missionary may be able to communicate. Among some AICs he may even find this to be a hitherto unknown quantity."[4] It was in the challenging context of AICs in Rhodesia that Inus Daneel found his calling.

Fluent in Shona from his childhood, Daneel had violated racial segregation by moving into the Shona communal lands in 1965; he lived there for three years, gaining the trust of traditional religious and black church leaders. One of the largest families of independent churches was called Zionist, named after Mount Zion in the Bible. For a period of time, Daneel lived in the holy "Zion" with Samuel Mutendi, founder of the largest branch: the Zion Christian Church. Mutendi had seventeen wives and many children. In long conversations over many years, the relationship became so close that Mutendi "adopted" Daneel as a son. During the liberation war, the white authorities tried to control Mutendi and his followers by arresting some of his sons. In solidarity with his adopted family, Daneel sat in the docket with the Mutendis throughout their trial, and then he bailed them out of jail with his own funds.

In 1972, in the midst of the civil war, Daneel and twelve AIC leaders founded the African Independent Church Conference (Fambidzano yamaKereke avaTema).[5] Fambidzano brought together around a hundred churches founded by African leaders for collaborative theological education and development projects in communal areas. Over the next decade, fifteen thousand people completed Fambidzano's two-year certificate program, instructed by Shona-speaking tutors traveling to rural extension centers. In addition to providing theological and leadership training, the ecumenical movement of AICs petitioned for membership in the Rhodesian Council of Churches. Because most of the AICs were polygamous, they were not allowed full membership in the council. But the ecumenical movement was accepted as an associate member.

As the head of Fambidzano, Daneel traveled back and forth into rural areas. This was a very dangerous occupation. Cars on the highway were a chief target of the guerilla movement. Daneel's personal friendships with rural black church leaders, as well as his theological convictions, caused him to put his loyalty to ecumenical interracial relationships above his white ethnic loyalty. Although most Rhodesian males agreed to serve in the army reserves, he refused to bear arms against the Shona people, whom he considered his congregation. He was called up and interrogated by Colonel George Hartley of the Rhodesian Front, accused of treason against the white cause, and threatened with imprisonment in the notorious Chikurubi Prison.

In the midst of the war, Daneel preached on mission to the white church in Fort Victoria, where he was an elder. Since the nearby black Reformed church in Mucheke township was a product of the mission, he suggested, as an act of interracial witness during the war, perhaps the two churches should hold a joint worship service, or at least send representatives one Sunday to each other's churches. In the middle of Daneel's sermon, a white farmer began pounding on the pew, saying in Afrikaans, "No black man will sit next to me!" About a quarter of the several hundred white congregants walked out of the church. It took months before the pastor could convince them to return to worship.[6]

Similarly caught in the middle were rural African Christian leaders who worked with Daneel for theological education by extension. Marxist-inspired guerillas suspected them of being sellouts. Jesus was considered the God of the white people, and rural Christians had to bury their Bibles to protect themselves. Freedom fighters would enter an area and subject the villagers to all-night *pungwe*, or confession meetings—a cross between a traditional all-night spiritual encounter with ancestral spirits and a Communist show trial. So-called witches and traitors would be exposed and killed. At the same time, Rhodesian soldiers tortured, interrogated, and killed suspected freedom fighters with ruthless efficiency. They moved into areas of suspected guerilla activity and burned down people's huts.

A chief leader of the ecumenical movement among the Shona AICs was Bishop Matteo Forridge, an elderly leader of the Zion Christian Church.[7] Daneel and Forridge became close friends. As they spent time together, Forridge taught Daneel to loosen up from his stiff Dutch Reformed ways, and taught him to dance alongside the Zionist men. Forridge was moved to embrace church unity by the priestly prayer of Jesus in John 17:21. When facing death, Jesus prayed that his disciples would be united "that they may all be one. As you, Father, are in me and I am in you, may they also be in us, so that the world may believe that you have sent me." On his own initiative, Forridge itinerated around the Chinombe chieftancy, preaching church unity to the leaders of different denominations. He brought together Shona church leaders to sponsor multifaith baptismal ceremonies. Catholic evangelists, Dutch Reformed leaders, and representatives of the different AICs came to the ecumenical outdoor baptisms so they could baptize members of their own denominations in the context of a unity service. During the war, people had different reasons for wanting to be baptized. Some were converted to Christianity and wished to join a particular church. Others needed cleansing from evil spirits, and to be seen publicly as someone who was not a witch or a wizard. So they sought baptism or rebaptism as a public witness. Thus village evangelists baptized those of their own denominations. Just as the great revivalist Billy Graham brought people together through a shared evangelistic meeting but then asked them to commit to a local church, so Bishop Forridge followed similar practices. He was an irenic leader who wished to relate positively to all Christians.

Such peaceful testimony was challenging yet very important during a civil war. Forridge and his wife completed the Fambidzano theological education course. In his day job, he rode a bicycle and delivered mail to the Dutch Reformed mission station from Chinombe.[8] But his core identity was as brave leader of African churches. As the war worsened, Forridge risked his life to carry the Bible and theology lessons back and forth from the Fambidzano headquarters to the villages in his area.

One day Bishop Forridge came home and found eight guerilla fighters waiting for him, demanding to see the papers he was carrying from the white man. The bishop expected the worst. But a miracle happened. The guerillas spent the afternoon reading the Bible lessons and then announced that the lessons were good. They, too, were Christians, and they volunteered to distribute the Bible lessons to opposition-controlled areas! Forridge's stature as a man of God was such that he asked the guerilla fighters not to target Daneel, and they honored his request. One day they attacked a convoy of white-driven vehicles; they let Daneel's car pass but took out the vehicle behind his. After the war, Daneel learned that Forridge had protected him when he traveled in the area.[9]

Then one day a bomb planted in the roadway near Forridge's church headquarters went off and blew up a Rhodesian patrol. The Rhodesian forces responded by burning down the village. Bishop Forridge rushed into his hut and was able to rescue only one thing: the certificates he and his wife had earned for theological training. The Rhodesian forces arrested Bishop Forridge and tortured him for weeks about his relationship with guerillas.

For refusing to give up their friendship across racial lines, and for working together in ecumenical cooperation for Bible training among the rural Shona villagers, both Daneel and Forridge paid a high price. Their Christian solidarity amid a racial war put them in danger from both sides. Daneel was shunned by fellow whites in the Dutch Reformed Church. They considered him a heretic for working with the African churches. He was accused of treason and was threatened with imprisonment. Forridge lost his home as well as his health and hearing from torture, and he endured the terrible stress of witnessing to his Christian faith in a context in which mere possession of a Bible could cause him to be killed under suspicion of collaborating with white people.

To be friends with a person of another race and culture is never easy. But to do it during the Zimbabwean liberation war, part of Cold War politics, was to testify with one's life to the words of Saint Paul in Galatians 3:28: "There is no longer Jew or Greek, there is no longer slave or free, there is no longer male and female; for all of you are one in Christ Jesus." What this story illustrates is that in a context of revolution, cross-cultural and cross-racial friendship is the most dangerous kind. People who live in mutuality across racial and ethnic divides are those who offend the "principalities and powers" (Eph. 6:12). Especially in cross-cultural relationships, to live in mutuality as Christian friends means opening oneself to being misunderstood and criticized by both sides. In situations of war, oppression, and scarcity, embracing diversity is an act of defiance—of refusing to accept the status quo of hatred and suspicion that blames problems on outsiders or the racial "other."

The Monday Night Group:
Friendship as Support for the Struggle

Before his death on the cross, Jesus talked to his disciples about the deep love that undergirds friendship. He told them, "No one has greater love than this, to lay down one's life for one's friends" (John 15:13). No doubt his words were meant to strengthen them for what lay ahead—both the struggle to survive the persecution and the hatred directed against them, and the struggle to persevere as a united community. To lay down one's life for one's friends does not necessarily mean dying for them. It may also mean living for them in disciplined fellowship. Friendship is not a "lone ranger" activity. It can be practiced only in relationship. As John Wesley and the early Methodists knew, to be in fellowship with other believers requires practicing friendship. And to practice friendship means caring for the community through prayer, Bible study, and emotional support. This kind of discipline gives friends the courage to reach out to others. The circle of friends then grows even larger.

Down through history, the core practices of Christian fellowship have given believers the courage to speak truth to power and to defend the innocent, even at risk to their own lives. The late 1960s were a bad period for democracy. Dictators around the world cynically manipulated American opinion to paint their enemies as Communists and to get funds and weapons from the United States. Militaries overthrew elected governments throughout Latin America. In South Korea, a military coup brought to power President Park Chung-hee, who violently suppressed dissent under the guise of protecting the country from North Korean Communism. In the Philippines, President Ferdinand Marcos accumulated property and money, then declared martial law in 1972. Pro-democracy activists were "salvaged" and "hamleted," euphemisms for being murdered or forcibly relocated. In 1965–66, the Indonesian military massacred between five hundred thousand and one million supposed Communists. While the United States fought the Vietnam War to stop Communism, authoritarian anti-Communist dictators flourished throughout Asia and Latin America. During this difficult period of history, the disciplines of friendship gave courage for the struggle for democracy.

In the book *More Than Witnesses*, a group of American Protestant missionaries have written of their time in South Korea during the 1960s and 1970s.[10] Their weekly Monday night fellowship group turned into a pro-democracy advocacy group, as reports increased of government atrocities against Koreans who supported democratization. Each week they met in one another's homes, prayed, and shared information collected during the week. Not coincidentally, a number of the missionaries were married to Koreans. Their loyalty to Korean democracy was personal. It reflected the interaction of their Christian faith with their love of the Korean people. Their weekly prayer and fellowship gathering gave them the moral and spiritual support they needed to befriend the Korean people in their struggles.

The missionary group included the American wives of Korean theologians. Faye knew nothing of Korea when she married her husband, Steve Moon, whom she had met at Hartford Seminary. Nevertheless, in 1961, she moved with him to Korea and settled in to raise a family. She did not set out to be "political," but her commitment to her husband required it. After the coup d'état by Park Chung-hee, Faye joined a group of missionaries that supported democratization. She and Steve lived in a Christian commune with other families. Then in 1974, Steve was fired from the university where he taught because of his support for minjung, or "people's," theology and was arrested for pro-democracy activities. The Monday night group of pro-democracy missionaries became Faye's support group. She wrote, "I didn't know how much I needed others' friendship and understanding, until I became a member of the Monday Night Group in Seoul."[11]

With the other wives of prisoners on trial, Faye Moon engaged in street protests, made purple shawls to sell to support the protests, and testified in 1976 about oppression in Korea before the Women's National Assembly of the Presbyterian Church (USA). For the two years her husband was imprisoned, she was followed by secret police. But she managed to use US communication channels to smuggle out information about oppression in Korea and information from pro-democracy missionaries, and to bring in information that helped the protesters. After having to flee to the United States, Faye returned five years later, supported by the Presbyterian Church (USA), to befriend Korean prostitutes outside the US Army bases there.

Marion Kim was another American woman married to a Korean Christian scholar, Kim Yong-Bock. Marion moved to Korea in 1969. After she learned Korean, she began editing theological statements by pro-democracy theologians, including her husband. In 1978, Marion began working for the National Council of Churches in Korea. In that capacity, she partnered with the Reverend Kim Kwan-Suk to translate pro-democracy resolutions and stories of human rights violations into English. The group compiled a major report about atrocities, put it into microfilm, and smuggled it out of the country with a representative of the World Council of Churches, which then published it in the West. President Jimmy Carter was able to use this human rights report to confront President Park, the Korean dictator, when he visited the United States in 1979.[12]

Marion's personal support came from the Monday night group of pro-democracy missionaries. In 1980, Marion's husband was in hiding from the military regime after having previously been arrested and nearly beaten to death. The Monday night group helped hide Yong-Bock. Marion's summary words about the Monday night group reveal the power of friendships in supporting struggles for justice: "It has helped me keep my faith in the goodness and power of the human spirit. It has helped me to realize we are one community across all kinds of boundaries. Together we have shared the experience of solidarity with the Korean people, learning from their courageous actions to transform their society. We have also learned from each other's compassionate acts as we tried to practice the two greatest commandments: 'Love God and love your neighbor.'"[13]

Methodist missionary Gene Mathews married his Korean wife, Insook, after his first term as a missionary. He, too, found spiritual and emotional sustenance in the Monday night group. He writes how his life was changed when, after the declaration of martial law in 1972, he befriended Koreans who had been tortured by their government. Mathews was watched by five different government agencies and eventually befriended the Korean CIA agent who checked on him daily for years. The most important moment of his advocacy occurred in 1975, when the Korean CIA arrested eight random Korean men and accused them of being the ringleaders of the "People's Revolutionary Party."[14] The men were terribly tortured, sentenced to death for treason, and then executed without being able to see their families. The Monday night group supported the wives of the eight innocent men during their yearlong ordeal, as well as the families of others sentenced to lengthy prison terms. After the eight men were executed, riot police fought their wives who were trying to take their husbands' bodies for burial. Participants in the Monday night group tried to support the heartbroken women. Mathews recalls one terrible incident:

> Several priests and missionaries locked elbows and surrounded a cluster of women in front of the hearse. . . . I watched in horror as the door of the hearse was jerked open and Song Sang-jin's wife was dragged kicking and screaming out onto the pavement. . . . I was bodily thrown back some distance but got back through the riot police to try to protect the mother and daughter.

The mother held onto the hearse bumper with her hand while a burly policeman kicked her arm with his combat boots. I foolishly grabbed his foot and up-ended him before being driven back again. As I was being tossed back, I saw a policeman pick up a woman missionary and fling her so hard she crashed into another woman and both tumbled into the gutter. . . . So I grabbed the policeman from behind, gave an enormous swing and very nearly succeeded in tumbling him. He jumped at me with his club but backed off when I folded my arms and stared him down.[15]

In his years of solidarity and advocacy with Koreans, Gene Mathews was inspired by the women who confronted the Korean government on behalf of their husbands and sons. Upon his retirement from missionary service in 1997, he had spent forty-one years in Korea. He writes, "During that time, I had laughed joyfully because my Korean friends found unflagging humor even in dark times. And I had wept bitter tears because the Koreans had also shared with me their deep sorrows. I still cry at times when sudden memories of their courage and sacrifice overcome me. Praise be to God."[16]

In 2005, the democratic government of Korea held another trial and exonerated the eight men who were executed on trumped-up charges. The entire incident of the "People's Revolutionary Party" had been fabricated by the Park government to enhance its own power. But cross-cultural friendship continued the witness against the false narratives constructed by the "principalities and powers."

Chris Rice and Spencer Perkins:
Friendship as Beloved Community

One of the high barriers to friendship is race—especially when race is defined by differences in economic and political power. Christian friends treat each other with respect and honesty, and ask and grant forgiveness when needed. But what if the friendship carries the heavy baggage of entrenched racial injustice? What if the external struggle of race, and its centuries of accumulated injustices and prejudices, constantly feeds the internal struggle? What if racial division continually festers and breaks out into new wounds?

For Americans, it has often been said, racism is the "original sin." Between the mid-1500s to mid-1800s, over ten million Africans were torn away from their families, chained together, and abused, crammed like sardines into the rough holds of wooden ships and sold in the Americas. Many of the "founding fathers" of the United States, including George Washington and Thomas Jefferson, were slaveholders. In the US Constitution, slaves were considered only three-fifths of a person; they couldn't vote, but their presence accrued to the voting power of their white male owners. The bloody Civil War, fought over slavery, killed more Americans than any other war in US history to date. Even so, the end of black slavery did not end racism. As society reconstituted itself in the late 1800s, statewide policies of separate but equal launched Jim Crow racial segregation. Despite some progress in literacy and church-based self-help movements, African Americans remained the poorest of the poor. Prejudice and violence kept them in their place at the bottom rung of the economic ladder.

After the Second World War, alongside other anticolonial and nationalist movements in Asia and Africa, the American civil rights movement erupted. African Americans were fed up with having to sit in the back of the bus if whites got on. Children were sick of second-class schools in inferior facilities. College students insisted on being served at the soda counter in Woolworth's. Freedom Riders rode buses from the North to help southern blacks claim their rights to vote. Amid the violence unleashed by white bigots, African Americans and their allies engaged in strikes, boycotts, marches, and legal challenges to "separate but equal."

During the civil rights movement, nobody summarized the vision of God's kingdom better than Baptist minister and human rights leader Dr. Martin Luther King Jr. In 1957, King addressed the Conference on Christian Faith and Human Relations in Nashville on the subject "The Role of the Church in Facing the Nation's Chief Moral Dilemma." Speaking of the nonviolent protests in the fight for racial equality, King said, "The end is reconciliation; the end is redemption; the end is the creation of the beloved community. It is this type of spirit and this type of love that can transform opposers into friends."[17] In King's "beloved community," sacrificial, cross-racial friendship stands as a sign pointing to the deeper meaning of Christian fellowship. Followers of Jesus need to build the beloved community as a witness to Christ's kingdom of shalom, of peace and justice, of equality and salvation. To do this requires justice. But reconciliation between black and white also requires concrete friendships across the color line.

To chart the internal dynamics of interracial friendships is not easy, because they are often hidden. People feel too vulnerable to share themselves fully—and they certainly don't wish to go public with the process! Some of the most revealing insights into the pilgrimage of interracial friendship are those of Spencer Perkins and Chris Rice. For more than a decade leading up to Spencer's untimely death of a heart attack in 1998, the two friends modeled reconciliation between black and white Americans. Not only did their families live in community with each other in racially segregated West Jackson, Mississippi, but Spencer and Chris also spoke together publicly about the inner dimensions of their friendship. They produced a moving book, *More Than Equals*, that describes their Christian witness to "racial healing for the sake of the Gospel."[18] They started the Reconcilers Fellowship as a national ministry for racial reconciliation.

Chris and Spencer had in common childhoods shaped by their parents' struggle for cross-cultural and interracial reconciliation. Chris Rice describes how his father's activism began as a young pastor when, in 1964, he went south during Freedom Summer to help register black voters and to support equal rights for African Americans. Then in 1966, as United Presbyterian missionaries, Sue and Randy Rice moved their family to Korea. There they joined the Monday night group. Chris's father was one of the several missionaries who led protests against the unjust arrest and execution of the eight so-called members of the "People's Revolutionary Party." Sue Rice, along with Faye Moon and others, helped the outcast mixed-race children of Korean women and American servicemen.

Spencer Perkins's parents were civil rights icons John and Vera Mae Perkins. John Perkins had grown up poor in Mississippi in a sharecropper family. In 1947, he moved to California after his brother Clyde, a World War II veteran, was killed by a policeman. (The family feared for John's safety.) In California, John Perkins started a family and also found Jesus Christ. The same year that Randy Rice answered God's call to join the civil rights movement, 1964, the Perkins family followed God's call and moved back to Mendenhall, Mississippi, as "missionaries" to poor people. John founded Voice of Calvary Ministries to teach the Bible. But as his vision expanded, God called him to a holistic ministry to empower poor African Americans at the grassroots level. The Perkinses supported voter registration, boycotts, and other efforts to bring legal equality to African Americans. With Vera Mae running a Head Start center, they began providing a range of social services in Mendenhall.

Because of his parents' Christian convictions, in 1966, Spencer Perkins and his siblings were some of the first African Americans to integrate formerly all-white schools. It was a miserable experience to be the first and only blacks in a previously all-white school. Spencer recalled that on the first day of school, he was called "nigger" several times before he had even attended his first class. During the time he spent at the school, nobody sat on either side of him.[19] He was only thirteen. The daily experiences of prejudice and unremitting persecution at the hands of their white classmates—and the lack of response by white authority figures—scarred the Perkins children for life.

Spencer recalls with pride his parents' leadership of resistance against unjust arrests of black children in his hometown. But the civil rights struggle of the 1960s was brutal. When Spencer was sixteen, John Perkins was viciously beaten in a jail in Brandon, Mississippi, when he went to rescue some black college students from unjust arrest. Although both Chris Rice's and Spencer Perkins's fathers had engaged in civil rights protests against unjust regimes, that Randy Rice was a white foreigner likely saved him from the racial hatred faced by John Perkins. To be an outsider coming into an unjust situation is not safe, but it does not carry the same risk as being one of the hometown oppressed who leads others. John and Vera Mae Perkins survived the 1960s civil rights movement, more convinced than ever that Jesus Christ was calling them to seek justice and promote reconciliation between blacks and whites. By the mid-1970s, through his interracial ministries and his publications, John Perkins had become a leading voice of racial reconciliation among evangelical Christians nationwide.[20]

The parallel pilgrimages of the Rice and Perkins families aligned in the early 1980s in the persons of Chris and Spencer. After graduating from college, the Perkinses' son Spencer had returned to Mississippi to work in his parents' ministries. The Voice of Calvary and related holistic ministries attracted young Christian volunteers to its vision of reconciliation and equality. Volunteers raised their own support and moved to Mississippi to live among the poor African American community. In 1981, one of these volunteers was Chris Rice, then a student at Middlebury College in Vermont. Although he had grown up in Korea, Chris's awareness of the entrenched racism against black Americans, especially in the Deep South, was minimal. What he experienced in Mississippi profoundly changed his life and his identity as a Christian. Instead of returning to college, he decided to stay in West Jackson and live in community with African Americans.

But living among and helping people is not the same as being in deep relationship with them. After two years, he realized that "I had lived in a black neighborhood, worked in a black-led ministry and worshipped in a majority-black church, but had not gained a single close black friend. I realized that I really didn't know these black people with whom I had worked and worshipped for two years."[21]

For Spencer, years of being hurt by white people had taken its toll. He was filled with anger, and he found it hard to trust. Then in 1983, the community blew up over issues of race. Despite the church and ministry being majority black, it seemed that white people had gradually moved into most of the leadership positions. For a ministry based on the empowering of black leadership, the situation was explosive. The ministry needed to reorient itself around black leadership. Feeling rejected, a lot of the white people left the ministry. But those who stayed, both black and white, determined to launch a new beginning for racial reconciliation based on deeper honesty and fellowship. The group developed new policies to make black leadership more possible, such as fund-raising for salary support for the African American staff.

One important path to interracial reconciliation in the Voice of Calvary community was the building of personal relationships across the racial divide. Spencer and his wife, Nancy, started a biracial Bible study and fellowship group. Chris and his future wife, Donna, joined. Through their weekly meetings, friendships started to grow. By July 1984, the group discerned that the next step in their quest for interracial reconciliation would be to form an intentional community. Three blacks, three whites, and their children founded a home they named Antioch.[22] By December 1985, they pooled their resources to buy two houses, shared their incomes, ate meals together, and paid for one of their members to do youth ministry in the neighborhood they hoped to transform. Chris Rice recalled six years later, "As blacks had become my friends, a strange thing had begun to happen. The more we trusted each other, the less race was an issue. Not only did I allow black people to speak to my life and weaknesses, but I had earned enough trust to speak to theirs."[23]

Through the process of living together, worshipping together, and committing themselves to racial reconciliation, Spencer and Chris became "more than equals." They became brothers, whose lives were so intertwined that even close friends would call them by each other's names.[24] They went on the road, sharing their struggles with interracial friendship and the task of reconciliation. They spoke to college students, church groups, and professional societies about their interracial friendship in Christ. Racial reconciliation requires intentionality, patience, small continuous steps, partnerships, and even living in each other's neighborhoods. As both Chris and Spencer learned from their parents, the family of Christ is bigger and more important than the supposed security and comfort of the nuclear family. And it takes risk to gain what is more important. In the words of famous missionary Jim Elliot, "He is no fool who gives up what he cannot keep to gain what he cannot lose."[25]

The writings and the presentations by Spencer and Chris moved many people who listened to what they had learned from their years together. Most important, together they explored the challenging inner processes necessary to move toward reconciliation. Chris needed to remove his "white blinders" of privilege and to remain in relationship while absorbing black anger. Spencer discovered the need to avoid cultural stereotypes and to learn the history and deeper meaning of oppressed people's actions—and to learn from people themselves. Learning to trust white people after a lifetime of betrayal was one of his struggles. Both of them learned that when one part of the body of Christ hurts, all parts hurt. The difficulty of their mutual engagement was summarized by a favorite quotation from African American evangelist Tom Skinner: "Racial reconciliation . . . is whites and blacks holding on to each other, not letting go, and doing surgery on each other."[26]

In chapter 19 of *More Than Equals*, Spencer discusses the meaning of his friendship with Chris through the idea of the "yokefellow." Usually a yoke is put around the necks of oxen to keep them moving in the same direction so that they can accomplish a common task. While friendship is important, it can be fickle. Friends come and go. While he and Chris liked each other, their commitment was more like marriage. They called this being "yokefellows." The yokefellows stay together for the higher purpose of the kingdom. Their relationship is based on respect, intentionality, and commitment to the end. Together they are stronger to accomplish their mission. "Though most friendships take work if they are to stay healthy," Spencer writes, "they don't have to have a reason outside themselves to exist. But yokefellows are headed in a common direction, toward a common goal. When one becomes good friends with a yokefellow, it's like adding icing to a cake."[27]

The secret to the "beloved community," as Spencer testified before his death, is grace. Grace to accept God's forgiveness and forgive one's oppressors. Grace to forgive. Grace to love. Grace "to be a way of life."[28]

Conclusion: Wrestling Jacob
and the Blessing of a New Name

As I reflect on these stories of friendship and struggle, I am reminded of Jacob wrestling the stranger. Through his persistence, despite exhaustion, uncertainty, and injury, Jacob greeted the new day blessed. He took on a new identity, new confidence, and a renewed relationship with God. This renewal neither solved all his problems nor eliminated the difficult circumstances in which he found himself. But he arose from his encounter able to face the challenges of another day.

As recounted in Genesis 32, Jacob was in a precarious position. He feared that his powerful brother Esau, flanked by four hundred armed men, would kill him and his family for having stolen his birthright when they were boys. Jacob sent his family to safety and found himself alone waiting for the day of reckoning. A man appeared, and they wrestled all night. When it became clear that Jacob would not let go, the stranger—likely an angel or messenger from God—touched Jacob's thigh and put it out of joint. Even so, Jacob would not let go until the man blessed him. The stranger asked his name. "Jacob," he replied. The stranger blessed him by telling him he would no longer be called Jacob but rather Israel, for "you have striven with God and with humans, and have prevailed" (Gen. 32:28). When asked by Jacob for his name, the stranger refused to tell him. After receiving his blessing,

Jacob renamed the place of encounter Peniel. As the sun rose, Jacob limped away to meet his brother.

In this biblical text, Jacob's situation is dire. He is confronted by powerful forces. He is fighting with God, who sends the mysterious stranger. And he is struggling with himself. He isolates himself, in fear but likely also in guilt and regret for having broken with his older brother years before. In this situation, he refuses to release the stranger, even though he is wounded. He insists on receiving a blessing from him. He gets his blessing, but unbidden, he also receives a new name. The very act of struggling with God's messenger gives him a new identity.

Many Christians have been drawn to this powerful story as a metaphor for their own spiritual and physical trials. Theologian Jürgen Moltmann, while a prisoner of war from 1945 to 1948, felt it speak to his existential situation: his uncertain future in a ruined country, his survivor's guilt, and his agony about the Holocaust. Like Jacob, Moltmann and the other German prisoners carried profound psychic, spiritual, and physical wounds. And yet he emerged blessed from his experience of prison camp, where he learned about God and studied theology. In the gracious friendship shown by the Scottish people in the area, and the fellowship of other Christians at the Swanwick meeting of the Student Christian Movement, Moltmann felt forgiven of the war guilt that haunted him. Most important, he met Jesus Christ. He recounts, "I began to understand the assailed Christ because I felt that he understood me: this was the divine brother in distress, who takes the prisoners with him on his way to resurrection. I began to summon up the courage to live again, seized by a great hope. . . . This early fellowship with Jesus, the brother in suffering and the redeemer from guilt, has never left me since."[29] The story of wrestling Jacob, with its combination of woundedness and blessing, gave meaning to Moltmann's own experience of being found by God and of receiving hope and joy.

Like Jürgen Moltmann, the friends in this chapter struggled mightily with evil forces beyond their control, with each other, and with their own guilty consciences. Like Jacob, they refused to let go. They were wounded—accused of treason, tortured, arrested, ridiculed, and generally misunderstood by both sides. Yet by not letting go either of the struggle or of each other, they faced the new day blessed. Their persistence revealed to them the loving nature of God, even in the midst of strife.

It strikes me also that Jacob's receiving a new name, and himself renaming the place of encounter, applies to the nature of Christian friendship. As friends come to know each other, through persistence and mutual struggle, their identities are formed anew. Through shared struggle, they bless each other. In mutuality across racial boundaries, for example, Spencer Perkins and Chris Rice saw themselves in a new light. They gave new names to the shared ministry that grew from their continued affirmation of unity in friendship. Some years after the Zimbabwean liberation war, the indigenous churches in Masvingo renamed Inus Daneel "Bishop Moses" to designate who he had become in relation to what they shared in wartime. Whether literally or metaphorically, giving and receiving new names testifies to how struggle among friends brings them to a new place that neither could have found alone.

The great lesson of struggle in friendship is that despite trauma, new discovery of God's love appears possible in the light of shared community. Inspired by his Korean friends, Gene Mathews's final words about their shared hardships were "Praise be to God." Jürgen Moltmann discovered fellowship with Jesus and with other Christians through his imprisonment.

Hymn writer Charles Wesley's verses "Wrestling Jacob," also known as "Come, O Thou Traveler Unknown," were considered by Isaac Watts to be "worth all the verses he himself had written."[30] In the hymn, Wesley imagines himself as Jacob, recounting in first person the fight to hold the stranger and repeatedly asking him his name. Finally, thigh wounded, Jacob rises above his pain and weakness and demands to know whom he wrestles. As the dawn breaks, it is revealed that the stranger is none other than Love. In the soaring words of "Wrestling Jacob," Charles Wesley testifies,

> I know thee, Savior, who thou art,
> Jesus, the feeble sinner's friend;
> Nor wilt thou with the night depart,
> But stay and love me to the end:
> Thy mercies never shall remove,
> Thy nature and thy name is Love.

CHAPTER 6

Celebration

Friendship and Joy

Adam lived here. He was a wonderful friend and
guide. Because of Adam's life and death we have
been gifted with peace, hope, love, and immense
gratitude.

—Henri Nouwen, *Adam: God's Beloved*

A few years ago, one of my colleagues retired. A professor
from Korea, he had capped off his career by teaching in the
United States for the last phase. As we gathered for the ban-
quet dinner, I chatted with a former missionary to Korea, now
retired and living in Maine. Years before, he and the professor
had worked together in Korea. "It is great you came for the
party," I commented. The missionary replied, "I wouldn't have
missed it. I would go to the ends of the earth for my friend."

And so we come to the last feature of friendship that I explore in this book: celebration. Friendship and joy are insep-
arable. We have seen that cross-cultural friendship requires
remaining so that God's presence is known. It can result in

exile, though with a broadening vision of the family of Christ. In times of struggle, friendships testify to God's grace and the promised kingdom. But throughout, friendship is a cause for celebration. The very definition of friendship is that of joy in relationship with others.

In cultures around the world, friendship stands as one of the highest values. The joy of friendship is so intimate and so personal that it is mostly invisible to history. It is hard to trace except through exceptionally frank personal letters and memoirs. And yet we all know that joy underlies the daily interactions among friends. Despite the challenges of human weakness, friendship is itself a form of celebration.

My favorite expression of the joy of cross-cultural friendship comes from Edwin Smith, a mission scholar, Bible translator, and founder of the journal *Africa*. Smith was one of the first Westerners to see African religions as vehicles of God's grace. Over many years in Zambia and South Africa, he forged relationships with Africans. The following quotation concludes his book *The Golden Stool*, published in 1926 as a plea for deeper understanding of African cultures.

> There hangs before me in the place of honour in my study the enlarged photograph of Mungalo—one of my friends to whom I dedicate this book. He was an old chief of the Ba-ila at Kasenga. . . . He remained pagan to the end, yet if ever two men loved each other they were Mungalo and myself. In a land where the term *mulongo* ("friend") is sacred, he and I were "friends." Nobody ever spoke to me of Mungalo by name: it was always "thy friend." I never spoke of him by name: it was always

"my friend," and everybody understood. I can hear even now his ringing tones as he announced himself outside my door by calling me: *Mulongwangu!* ("my friend"); and can see his rugged countenance lighten as he welcomed me to his home with the same word: *Mulongwangu!* Heaven itself will be something less than heaven if I do not hear that greeting—*Mulongwangu!*—when I enter the pearly gates. We spent long hours together, whether in his hut, or in my study, or out in the open. He was a rare companion—the best raconteur I ever knew. We talked freely and frankly, discussing all things on earth and in heaven, so far as our limited experience would allow. Pagan as he was, I rarely have known a man of finer reverence. He was deeply religious. . . . Anyone who has enjoyed the intimate friendship of one African can never think meanly of the race. They have a genius for friendship; they excel in loyalty. No people perhaps are more capable of a deep and constant fidelity to those whom they love—for their sake they will go through fire and water and brave a thousand deaths.[1]

Smith's celebration of Mungalo does not confine friendship to other Christians. In fact, his friendship with Mungalo deepens his appreciation for other Africans as well. Joyful relationships that cross cultures are not limited to those who think, live, and believe exactly the same. And yet those friendships still provide strength for the journey and testify to God who loves the whole world. Smith could not imagine heaven without his beloved friend Mungalo, even though Mungalo was not a believer. His words reflect some of the paternalism of the colonialist 1920s, yet his delight in his friend radiates throughout. Smith knew the truths expressed by Spencer Perkins and Chris Rice in the last chapter—that a secret to respecting the humanity and gifts of persons of other races or cultures lies in concrete friendship with particular persons.

In this chapter, I explore two case studies of embracing diversity through friendship. In each story, relationships culminate in celebrations of life. And those celebrations had impact beyond the friendships themselves. Joy in friendship across profound differences can result from following the way of Jesus Christ in the world. Yet these stories also reveal that the joy of cross-cultural friendship is not confined to relationships with other Christians.

First is the example of American missionary Frank Laubach, who worked among the Muslim Moros in the Philippines. His friendship with them resulted in the celebration of cultural empowerment and religious devotion. It also culminated in a worldwide movement to teach illiterates to read. The second example explores the work of famed Dutch spiritual writer Henri Nouwen, and his huge capacity for friendship. In particular, his friendship with a severely disabled Canadian named Adam illuminated pathways to a deeper, joyous relationship with God. Although Laubach was a Protestant and Nouwen a Catholic, they were both mystics who saw the face of God shining in people whom they initially assumed were unlike themselves.

Frank Laubach, the Moros of the Philippines, and International Literacy

In his book *Letters by a Modern Mystic*, Frank Laubach writes, "Knowing God better and better is an achievement of friendship."[2] Written between 1930 and 1932 near Lake Lanao in the Philippines, the letters reflect Laubach's efforts to keep God in the center of his thoughts at all times. In his delight at God's presence, Laubach compares knowing God to falling in love and losing oneself in the other. To merely believe in God is not enough; even devils believe in God. To be acquainted with God is not enough, for acquaintance is like doing business with someone. To Laubach, loving God meant being God's friend.

Laubach mused that friendship is formed by "doing things together."[3] It requires growth, or else it stagnates. Just as the child loves the parent and gradually becomes like him, "so we may grow into closer love with God by widening into his interests, and thinking His thoughts and sharing His enterprises."[4] Through helping God in the world, and walking and talking with him, "God simply creeps in and you *know* He is here in your heart. He has become your friend by working along with you."[5]

Frank Laubach linked his friendship with God to his friendship with the Moro people. His mystical awareness of God's presence occurred at the same time he was trying to relate to them. He grew keenly aware of the spiritual connection he shared with devout Moros. Out of this connection grew one of the most important world literacy movements of the twentieth century. But Laubach's preparation for his friendship with the Moros began years before he moved among them. It all began in 1912, when he and his new wife, Effa, felt called to become missionaries on the island of Mindanao in the Philippines. After his graduation from Union Theological Seminary in New York, Laubach was appointed a Congregationalist missionary. At that time, the Philippines was a United States colony. The island nation had been claimed by the US in 1898, during the brief Spanish-American War. Additional, brutal armed conflict lasting until 1902, known as the Filipino-American War, solidified American control but killed a large percentage of the Filipino people. The flip side of the US-Filipino relationship, however, involved social transformation, including widespread education and land reform. In 1901, over a thousand American schoolteachers were sent to the Philippines, sponsored by the US government. The teachers were tasked to build schools and establish a modern educational system that included the teaching of English. The Laubachs knew two of these teachers. So their missionary call to the Philippines combined motives of spiritual and physical uplift, nested in the context of American imperialism.

From 1919 to 1922, the Laubachs were on furlough at Union Theological Seminary. There Frank studied with Daniel Fleming, one of the most perceptive and progressive Protestant mission theorists at the time. He discovered the problem of illiteracy in Fleming's new book, *Marks of a World Christian*: at least three-fifths of the world was illiterate, and, especially in a rapidly modernizing world, illiterates were shut out from power and resources, and victimized by social forces controlled by those who were more educated. Also by this time, Laubach was convinced of the strategic importance of Filipino Christians in world evangelization. The Philippines was the only Asian Christian nation, which uniquely situated the diaspora Filipino population to evangelize Asia. In a book on Filipino religious history that grew from his research at Union and was published in 1925, Laubach argues that Filipino Christianity could lead the way in the indigenization of the faith—in launching a Christianity freed from oppressive Western control or influence.[6] He believed that with their cultural knowledge of both East and West, Filipino Christians could bridge the chasm between the two.

In 1929, Laubach finally was appointed to work among the Moros. After leaving his wife and child north of Manila, he went by himself. Life among the Moros was dangerous. A Muslim ethnic group that had never been defeated by the Spanish, the Moros had similarly fought against the Americans during the Filipino war against the United States. They were subdued by General John Pershing, but they resented American and Filipino control and opposed the Christian religion. They surely did not want a do-gooder American missionary living among them at Lake Lanao.

Laubach recounts that the year of 1929 was the loneliest and most discouraging of his entire life. Every evening, when other expats were drowning their loneliness in heavy drink, Laubach climbed a hill to pray. After a month of prayer, sitting on the hilltop, he heard a message from God. God told him he was a failure because he did not truly love the Moros. He felt superior to them because he was a white American. If only he would love them, they would love him back. He acknowledged to God the truth of this accusation. With his lips moving seemingly beyond his control, Laubach felt God say to him, "If you want the Moros to be fair to your religion, be fair to theirs. Study their Koran with them."[7] This transformative moment on the hilltop, a mystical experience of knowing God's will, gave Laubach the courage to deepen his engagement with the religious and cultural "other."

The following several years consisted of steady exchanges of views, joint study, and deepening friendship between Frank Laubach and the Moro people. As he read the Qur'an with them, he discovered the important place Jesus holds in it. He learned of their tradition that next to the grave of Muhammad lies an empty grave for Jesus, who will one day return and judge the people. After a thousand-year reign, Jesus would be buried alongside Muhammad.[8]

Laubach also began studying the Moro language and culture. He became close friends with a man named Pambaya. They worked closely together on a Moro-English dictionary. Laubach and his team translated parts of the Bible into Maranaw, including Luke and the book of Acts. With a donated printing press, they printed the first pages ever written of the Moro language in roman letters. Laubach made it his mission to preserve as much of the Moro sung poetry as he could by writing it down. He and Moro partner Gani Noor also translated Moro classics into English, such as the epic song of the Moro ancestral hero Bantugan.

To engage a wider group, Laubach and Pambaya started a newspaper with material about Moro culture, such as the stories of the ancestors. The paper was also practical, as it contained information relevant to trade and agriculture. The first issue was printed in 1930. The printing of the Moro language in a romanized script opened the desire of the people to learn to read. Prior to Laubach's romanization of the Moros' language, their literacy was limited by the use of a difficult arabic script. So Laubach began experimenting with a literacy campaign. As he wrote to his father,

> Now we have to teach everybody how to read the paper. . . . We have prepared a chart full of short sentences with very large letters. . . . We asked the Moros to help us and tried out all the ideas that they submitted. They are helping us to look for "key words" that will contain all their twelve consonants. They found some rather good "keys," but we are seeking better ones. We keep telling ourselves that this chart must be worked over like an automobile road, until every step is smooth and the grade so easy that the poorest car could slip along without getting stuck or even jolted.[9]

Through constant experimentation and honing of his method, by 1932, Laubach and his team were producing three thousand newly literate adults a month. His method began spreading throughout the Philippines and beyond. Then in 1935, he departed for his first world tour to spread his literacy method.

Laubach shared the importance of friendship in the development of his method in a student address and radio interview he gave during his first world tour. He advised theology students how to be "real." The only way he knew, he said, was "to go down into the slums of the city, as Jane Addams did, or as Kagawa did in Kobe, Japan, and let human need break your heart. Then when you preach, people will know you are real. You cannot help other sufferers until you have suffered yourself."[10]

In teaching the Moros to read, Laubach "discovered that teaching a man to read is a wonderful way to win his friendship."[11] A small team of supporters led by the Moro linguist Gani Noor traveled the country, telling people that Laubach was their friend and inviting them to learn to read.[12] In a letter to his father, Laubach shared his response to a pious Muslim man (a hajji who had visited Mecca) who asked him why he was helping the Moros. He had replied that the Moros needed a friend, and that he was also learning from them: "You have been helping me in Lanao, for here I have learned that 'Moslem' means 'one who does the will of God in every smallest detail,' and since I have been here I have been trying harder than ever before in my life to keep God in my mind all day. Whenever I find a man like yourself who is trying to submit to the will of God, then he is my dearest friend. You and I shall be friends forever."[13] Laubach sought similarities between the teachings of Muhammad and Jesus, such as the importance of doing God's will.[14] Through shared spiritual understanding, Laubach also drew closer to the divine. The mutuality of this friendship was expressed repeatedly by Moro leaders, who honored Laubach as one of their own and even turned to him for religious leadership. As one told him, "We hope that you will promise to live among us forever. We will write our friendship upon iron."[15]

When mission money to pay literacy teachers dried up, one local chief came up with the idea that each learner should commit himself to teach others. If each person who learned to read would teach someone else for free, the movement for literacy could continue indefinitely. Laubach named this method "Each One Teach One." When the Laubachs left the Moros to go abroad, he recalled:

> Four truckloads of Moro priests and datos and sultans followed us to the sea coast. They crowded the deck. After they had made speeches awhile they selected the chief imam to pray. Very reverently they held out their hands as they prayed that this American friend whom they had helped to make the easiest method of teaching in the world should have the blessing of Allah as he started across the world teaching the MORO method to all the illiterate nations of the world. They all wanted to go with me! As they kissed me good bye with their Arab whiskers many of them wept as they said: "We will pray for you in every mosque in Lanao."
>
> Then they bowed reverently as our Christian church members prayed and sang: "God be with you till we meet again."[16]

Around the world, missionaries and indigenous workers gathered to learn the method Laubach had developed in close relationship with the Moros. His correspondence and newsletters show how his mystical unity with God and his love for the Moros launched a wide network of passionate workers for worldwide literacy. Laubach considered his literacy movement a form of empowerment and a counterwitness to racism. He warned prospective missionaries that racial exclusivism by Westerners creates a burden of hypocrisy that undercuts the spread of the gospel. His passion to teach the illiterate billion people of the world grew from his deep commitment to "abundant life" for all.[17] By the time he died in 1970, Frank Laubach had introduced the Each One Teach One and keyword methods into 103 countries and 313 languages. Networks of literacy advocates, many mobilized by churches, sponsored his method in countries around the world.

The story of Frank Laubach's relationship with the Moros and their shared commitment to God is a celebration of friendship. Ever the optimist, in his autobiography, *Thirty Years with the Silent Billion*, he mentions he hoped to write a tract series called "Jesus as a Good Friend."[18] In this way, perhaps the respect of the Muslim Moros for Jesus could be separated from their centuries of enmity with Western Christendom.

History has not been kind to the relationship between the Moros and the majority of non-Muslim Filipinos. The Moros remain in conflict with the government of the Philippines. Misunderstandings, conflicts, and differences abound. Yet Frank Laubach's words continue to provide hope: "I never had friends whom I felt I could rely upon to be more loyal and who understood my own motives better than the Moros. Neither they nor I feel that the boundary of religion or race can keep us apart."[19]

Henri Nouwen, Adam Arnett, and the Search for Home

When the ancient philosophers talked about friendship, they assumed it was a relationship between equals. Like seeks like, and the most effective friendships are those crafted around shared interests, perspectives, and understandings—as well as underlying similarities in social class, education, gender, and other factors. As this book has shown, however, the Christian vision of friendship is different. If friends are anchored in Christ, then cultural and class similarity is not required for friendship. Transnational, cross-cultural, and other boundary-crossing relationships become possible when both parties relate to each other through their Christian faith. And as the example of Frank Laubach shows, joyous relationships between friends can also be interreligious, especially when a Christian love ethic self-consciously underlies the effort to make friends.

This next story of friendship as joy is unusual because, on the surface, the two friends were profoundly unequal. One was the famed Dutch Catholic priest Henri Nouwen, who wrote over forty books, many of them best sellers translated into multiple languages. He was a highly educated and cultured man. He was a psychologist and a theologian, a professor at Yale and, later, Harvard, and a popular speaker on several continents. He loved Rembrandt and maintained an active interest in religion and the arts. The other friend was the profoundly disabled Canadian young man Adam Arnett, who could not speak or verbally respond. Adam's life was confined to his family home and to institutions. The boundaries between him and Henri were huge. Yet for Henri, Adam was a dear friend. Henri wrote, "I love him, and our relationship was one of the most significant of my life. Adam's death touched me deeply because for me he was the one who more than any book or professor led me to the person of Jesus."[20]

Henri celebrated his friendship with Adam in one of his last books, *Adam: God's Beloved*. The intimate story of their relationship raises important issues about the nature of friendship. Can it exist when the friends are unable to communicate verbally back and forth? Can friendship exist when the relationship is based on physical care rather than shared interests? Certainly Henri Nouwen thought so. The story of Henri and Adam is as profound a story of embracing diversity as that of Frank Laubach and the Muslim Moros. It begins with the assumption of utter dissimilarity between the two parties and, through a process of deepening friendship, ends with affirmation of their similarities. A shared spiritual identity, grounded in Christ, goes beyond words. Friendship is a matter of being as well as doing, and Henri and Adam remind us of just that—that underneath everyone lies an almost instinctive claim of shared humanity that may not depend on the usual list of qualities one seeks in a friend.

My interest in this story is personal, as I counted Henri Nouwen first as a teacher and then as a friend. When I went to Yale Divinity School in the fall of 1978, I enrolled in his course on Thomas Merton. I had written my undergraduate thesis on the Jesuit activist Daniel Berrigan. Through Berrigan, I had discovered Merton, the Trappist monk and author of spiritual classics on contemplative prayer and the relationship between faith and action. Henri's classes allowed me to immerse myself in Merton's spiritual writings, as well as to pray regularly in a small group. Henri's assistant, John Mogabgab, later head of Upper Room Ministries, mentored our small group in contemplative prayer.

After the course ended, I got to know Henri better. In August 1982, my fiancé, Bob Massie, and I went with some of Henri's other friends, former students, and relatives to the Trappist Abbey of the Genesee in upstate New York. There, over a couple of days, we celebrated the twenty-fifth anniversary of Henri's ordination to the priesthood. Our friendship with Henri deepened when, in November, he traveled to Baton Rouge to marry us. (His sermon on John 15 later fed into his book *Lifesigns*.) While Bob and I were on our honeymoon, Henri stayed with my parents and enjoyed visiting the chemical plant where my father worked. I still treasure a photo of Henri in a hard hat, touring the Dow Chemical plant in Plaquemine, Louisiana, with my father.

By 1984, Henri was teaching at Harvard Divinity School, and I was teaching at the Boston University School of Theology. So Bob and I saw him regularly for meals and visits. Henri had arranged with Harvard to spend six months in South America and six months teaching. This arrangement was not an entirely happy experience for him. As a Catholic priest, Henri was the object of scorn by students at Harvard Divinity School who saw him as a symbol of patriarchy.

Then in the summer of 1985, Bob, Henri, and I went on pilgrimage together to Russia. As Russians prepared to celebrate a thousand years of Russian Orthodoxy, the Orthodox Church of America arranged with the Russian Orthodox Church to bring a trial group of pilgrims to test out the church's ability to host large groups during the 1986 centennial. The three of us joined this group. We visited monasteries, spoke with seminarians, and venerated a lot of relics. We even got to meet Patriarch Pimen during a festival at Danilov Monastery. I have vivid memories of walking and chatting with Henri in Moscow. As his relationship with the disabled was beginning, he showed extra sensitivity to the health needs of my husband, who was a hemophiliac. Henri insisted on pushing Bob's wheelchair across the rough pavement in Moscow and Saint Petersburg.

The highlight of the trip for Henri was when we got permission to enter the State Hermitage Museum in Saint Petersburg on a day it is normally closed. This was arranged by Bob's mother, Suzanne Massie, who was a friend of the curator's. One of Henri's chief motivations for traveling to Russia was to see Rembrandt's painting *Return of the Prodigal Son*. It had been hidden behind the Iron Curtain for many decades, and good reproductions of it did not exist in the West. As we rounded the corner and stood before the huge, magnificent Rembrandt, Henri was overwhelmed with emotion. "I didn't know there was an elder son," he exclaimed upon seeing the angry face of the older brother observing his father forgiving the younger son for his wayward life. Henri was given permission to spend a full day sitting in front of Rembrandt's masterpiece. The resultant reflection became one of his most-loved books, *The Return of the Prodigal Son*.[21]

As someone who knew Henri Nouwen, I agree with what others have observed. Henri had a huge capacity for friendship. He loved people. He corresponded with friends, remembered their birthdays, and sent them gifts on special occasions. He was also achingly lonely and asked a lot of his friends, often more than they could provide.

One core theme throughout Henri Nouwen's writings and ministry was his deep longing for intimate relationship. As a Catholic priest, he was limited in his physical interactions with others. The priestly requirement of celibacy required a certain disconnectedness from one's own physical body, including the physical tasks of life such as hands-on care for others and mundane tasks such as housework. To be a writer and a teacher also required isolation. The separation required by priests in order to fulfill their sacramental roles and the price of scholarship were both accepted by him as part of his ministry. Given the isolation of celibate priesthood, Henri's search for a physical and spiritual home was one of the inspirations for some of his most self-revealing and sensitive writings about the nature of the spiritual life. To be a spiritual guide for millions required plumbing the depths of one's own loneliness and isolation. Repeatedly he was thrown into dependence on God for his very existence.

Henri's longing for home turned into a homecoming when, in August 1986, he moved to Daybreak, a residential community for the disabled in Toronto. Daybreak was one of the L'Arche (French for "ark") homes founded by Jean Vanier, who opened the first one in 1964 in Trosly-Breuil, France. His motivation was to do good for "the least of these," through whom Jesus himself could be known. Vanier recalled his first relationships with the disabled: "Essentially, they wanted a friend. They were not very interested in my knowledge or my ability to do things, but rather they needed my heart and my being."[22] As his vision spread, L'Arche communities opened in thirty-seven countries as havens for the disabled and their caregivers, who lived together in mutuality. Vanier believed in breaking down the barriers that separated the developmentally disabled from others. In this, he followed Jesus in a life of love in hopes that all would become "a beloved friend of Jesus."[23]

Upon moving to Daybreak, Henri was assigned to the morning routine for Adam, who required around-the-clock care. Adam was born in 1961 with severe epilepsy. Because of overmedication after a seizure, he lost what little ability he had to move around. Nor could he speak or respond. His loving parents took care of him and his disabled older brother as long as they could. Even after moving Adam to a hospital for the chronically disabled, his parents spent five years looking for a more humane and loving situation for their son. Once it was decided to place him at Daybreak, it took more than a year to prepare the place. Adam needed to be fed, dressed, toileted, shaved, cared for during the day, and then made ready for bed at nighttime. Caregivers had to be trained, the facilities modified, and arrangements made for seamless transitions and potential medical emergencies.

Henri was overwhelmed at being assigned to handle Adam's morning routine. There he was, an intellectual, assigned to the most challenging resident at Daybreak. Henri knew nothing about feeding, changing, and physically caring for a person who could not give verbal clues about his needs. Henri recalls that when he started caring for Adam, he focused on learning the routine. As an incredibly busy person, Henri initially thought of Adam as a project to get through before he could start his real work of reading, writing, speaking, and the like. He expected no communication and rather saw Adam as a project to be mastered. He felt as if he and Adam had nothing in common. But as with other kinds of cross-cultural immersion, over time, Henri's relationship with Adam deepened. He mastered the routine and moved on to deeper forms of engagement. He started talking to him, even though he got no response—not even a smile. He started reading signs in Adam's demeanor, such as the seizures that came if Henri rushed the routine or did it wrong.

Bit by bit, things changed. As he got in closer touch with Adam's "language," Henri found his own identity was being transformed in relationship to Adam. Henri wrote, "We were together, growing in friendship, and I was glad to be there. Before long Adam became my much trusted listener."[24] Henri shared his secrets with him and gradually realized that "Adam was really there for me, listening with his whole being and offering me a safe space to be." As time went on, "I grew attached to my one or two hours a day with Adam. They became my quiet hours, the most reflective and intimate time of the day. Indeed they became like a long prayer time." Henri started thinking about Adam during the day as a "silent, peaceful presence in the center of my life."[25]

Adam, in short, was becoming Henri's friend. "I started to experience a true relationship with and love for Adam. Adam now was no longer a stranger to me. He was becoming a friend and a trustworthy companion, explaining to me by his very presence what I should have known all along: that what I most desire in life—love, friendship, community, and a deep sense of belonging—I was finding with him."[26] As Henri took care of Adam, he rediscovered and became more rooted in his own physical being. In Henri's eyes, Adam went from being a foreigner to part of himself. What had started as an unfamiliar way of being became the place where Henri felt at home. And Adam knew that Henri loved him.

Henri Nouwen came to see Adam as an emissary of Christ. As his friend and brother, Adam became for Henri a messenger of God's love. Their "spiritual bonding" meant that, like true friends, they were total equals. Difference had become transformed into personal identification. Adam even became to Henri a missionary, announcing the good news.[27] And Henri needed to receive healing from him.

For fourteen months, Henri cared for Adam on a daily basis. Then he became the official chaplain at Daybreak. As his role changed, the transition marked a new phase of their relationship. "Now we could be friends, members of the same community, two men journeying together to God. Our poverties had touched each other and our relationship was sound."[28] Adam had taught him how to give *and* how to receive.

In February 1996, Adam died at age thirty-four. After his funeral, Henri was plunged into grief. The joy of friendship had given way to the pain of loss, the sense of life's futility, and the seeming permanence of death. But from the pain came the stirrings of resurrection. People at Daybreak began dreaming about Adam—a vibrant Adam who could speak, walk, and even dance. Henri began telling Adam's story. Just as Jesus's disciples found new hope in telling stories of the resurrection, so did stories of Adam's vulnerability and presence on earth bring hope. "Mourning turns to dancing, grief turns to joy, despair turns to hope, and fear turns to love. Then hesitantly someone is saying, 'He is risen, he is risen indeed.'"[29] And so from Adam's death, in the midst of grief, came the mystery of new life.

Henri Nouwen closed his book with these words: "Adam lived here. He was a wonderful friend and guide. Because of Adam's life and death we have been gifted with peace, hope, love, and immense gratitude."[30] Seven months after Adam's death, Henri himself died suddenly of a heart attack. As with Jesus and Adam, those blessed to have been Henri's friends glimpse the joy of resurrection through talking and writing about him.

Conclusion: Celebration, Gratitude, and New Life

The stories in this chapter show how joyous friendship cuts across the boundaries of differing cultures, religions, and abilities. They also show that faithful friendships extend themselves through gratitude. We know the stories of Frank Laubach and the Moros, and of Henri and Adam, because gratitude led to their being remembered and shared. Frank Laubach's literacy campaign became possible when he allowed God's love for the Moros to overcome his own judgmentalism about their religious and cultural differences. Henri Nouwen found himself becoming whole when he celebrated Adam's special gifts. Friendship includes celebration. And celebration nurtures thankfulness. And the spirit of gratitude ripples across time and space, opening hearts to possibilities of new life. Thanksgiving and gratitude are essential to the mutual openness that characterizes joyous friendships.

I would argue that gratitude provides an important link between the classical views of friendship as a recognition of virtue in the other and Christian views of love for God and neighbor. Friends' gratitude for the friendship they share demonstrates appreciation for the good they see in each other . True friends help each other cultivate the best in themselves.[31] For Christians, gratitude not only encourages personal virtue but also responds to God's offer of friendship through Jesus Christ.

In the seventeenth chapter of Luke, the Gospel writer records that ten lepers went to Jesus and asked to be healed. And so he healed them. But the main point of the story is not the healing. The main point is that only one turned back to express his gratitude. Ten lepers accepted what Jesus could do for them. However, nine closed off the possibility of friendship with Jesus because they did not reciprocate with the mutuality of thanksgiving. After they were healed, they took him for granted. No doubt the lepers were eager to be reunited with their families after suffering the alienation of disease for so long. But they didn't wait long enough even to give thanks. As in modern society, they were too busy with their lives to bother.

When the single leper returned, he praised God with a loud voice. He "fell on his face at Jesus's feet, giving him thanks." Ironically, the thankful leper was a Samaritan—the only "foreigner" of the bunch. Only the foreigner expressed mutuality through gratitude, thanking Jesus. While the text does not tell us that Jesus and the Samaritan became friends, the Samaritan's expression of gratitude opened up the possibility of further relationship. It certainly increased his joy in his healing, and Jesus's joy in healing him. Jesus told the man to rise—a sign of equality—and to get on with his life. Gratitude to God and joy at being healed were responses that transcended the cultural and religious differences that divided the Jewish Jesus from the Samaritan leper.

In her book *Joyful Witness in the Muslim World*, Evelynne Reisacher emphasizes how joy flows from friendships with persons of different religions and cultures than one's own. She has reached that conclusion after many years of friendship with Muslims. Reisacher links biblical joy and joy in God to her joyous relationships with individual Muslims. Reisacher suggests that the first step toward relating to Muslims is to enjoy them "as human beings."[32] Celebration of common humanity is the basis for overcoming stereotypes and divisions, despite the challenges of cultural and religious differences.

Like Spencer Perkins, Chris Rice, and Edwin Smith, Reisacher argues that attachment to specific persons will help overcome prejudices against whole populations.[33] Thus concrete friendships are the first step toward both acceptance of an entire group of people and sharing love in Jesus Christ. Reisacher asks a provocative question: If Jesus were telling the story of the good Samaritan today, would the good Samaritan be a Muslim?[34] Given the common virtues of Muslims and Christians, including care for the poor and hospitality, joyous friendship is possible on a personal level. The sharing of ordinary living is often called the "dialogue of life." Reisacher quotes Johannes Verkuyl, who notes that the "dialogue of life consists of 'interreligious encounters founded in deep, personal and lasting friendships . . . where heart meets heart.'"[35] She recounts, as an example, the friendship of a Christian woman named Michal and a Muslim woman named Sondos. They read the Bible and the Qur'an together, "laugh and cry at life's twists and turns, and foster a deeper understanding of God's purpose for them."[36]

In her book, Reisacher underscores the concrete benefits of joy, which has much more to offer than fear and insecurity. Scientific studies show that joy is a psychologically healthy behavior. It is intrinsically relational, and it grows when spread from one person to another. Reisacher argues that relational joy flows from the triune God. It is an essential part of Christian identity and witness.

Delight, joy, celebration . . . these are qualities of friendship that allow Christians to bridge differences in love for others—differences that seem profound at first, but that melt away in light of our common, God-given humanity. As the biblical virtue of gratitude flows out from our friendships, it waters new life. And the mustard seed of friendship grows into a big tree.

CHAPTER 7

Christian Friendship Today

Mustard Seeds of Hope

I have seen things change. I have seen people
change. . . . I've changed.

—Daryl Davis, *Accidental Courtesy*

In downtown Houston, Rudy and Juanita Rasmus pastor
St. John's United Methodist Church. Starting with nine people
in 1992, the church grew into a dynamic, multiracial ministry
that embraces people of all economic and social groups. Rudy
Rasmus writes, "Friendships are the power of ministry. I'm
just a guy with a smile on my face, passing a piece of bread
and a bowl of soup to a friend."[1] When he names friendship as
the "power of ministry," it sounds simple and straightforward.
But his statement is only the tip of the iceberg of a homeless
ministry called Bread of Life. Befriending the homeless alerted
Rasmus to their needs. In addition to meals, they wanted a
place to take showers, receive medical care, and find help for
substance abuse. Now St. John's outreach includes housing assistance, an employment agency, and anti-hunger initiatives.[2]

What started as simple friendship across racial and economic boundaries has blossomed into a transformational ministry.

Throughout this book, I have made the bold claim that down through history, faithful friendship is like the mustard seed of Jesus's parable. The Gospel of Matthew records Jesus explaining the kingdom of heaven. One way he describes it is by way of analogy to the mustard seed. Even though it is sown as only a tiny seed, "when it has grown it is the greatest of shrubs and becomes a tree, so that the birds of the air come and make nests in its branches" (Matt. 13:32) As with Rudy Rasmus and his church's ministry to Houston's homeless, the life stories in this book show that friendship starts small and close to the ground. It needs soil, sun, and water to grow. It takes a long time. But the roots of the mature tree stabilize it, and its branches support other life.

From the time of Jesus and the disciples, friendships have undergirded the witnessing community of Christ. Friendship is a biblical practice, essential to the mission of the church. The evidence for this does not lie in structures or formal doctrines. In fact, theologians have often commented that personal friendship can be a distraction from the larger church community and can compete with it. Evidence for the importance of friendship comes, instead, from the life narratives of people of faith. As believers reach across cultural, political, and social boundaries in the name of Christ, they forge relationships of equality and care that are signposts of the kingdom of God.

Throughout the history of Christianity, boundary-crossing believers have reflected on the meaning of friendship, especially as they've enacted it. From this discourse has evolved the understanding that friendship integrates being and do-ing: if I am your friend in Christ, my identity evolves in rela-tionship to yours. And to be your friend, I must act like one. Together, we create a chain of relationships, a network of Jesus's followers who share our friendship with one another because we are united in him. Jesus's words about friendship give us the courage to reach beyond ourselves to help others, to witness, and to love people we might not normally love. Thus the practice of faithful friendship is an end in itself. It is not a means to an end, even though it often carries important consequences. It is not a project or a technique. It is often hidden to history. When we catch glimpses of it, as in the stories in this book, we stand amazed at its trans-formative power.

Stories of cross-cultural friendship show how love and compassion can broaden the notion of family. Being a friend is at the same time very ordinary and the stuff of miracles. When things are the worst and life is the hardest, friendships in Christ take on heightened importance. Cross-cultural friendship is essential for building community, pursuing justice, and making peace. Friendships witness against systems built on hatred and division. Young people yearn for friendship with others unlike themselves, and in this lies hope for the future. Friendship seeds fellowship, and fellowship points to the kingdom of God. In pointing to shalom—the vision of peace, salvation, and justice about which Jesus spoke—friendship carries in its core the joy of resurrection.

Limitations and Challenges
of Christian Friendship Today

Depictions of the kingdom of God often turn to Isaiah 11:6–7 for inspiration. From the dozens of *Peaceable Kingdom* paintings by nineteenth-century Quaker Edward Hicks to modern poster art, the image of a lion and a lamb being led by a little child envisions the peacefulness and equality of God's future reign. The text reads,

> The wolf shall live with the lamb,
>> the leopard shall lie down with the kid,
> the calf and the lion and the fatling together,
>> and a little child shall lead them.
> The cow and the bear shall graze,
>> their young shall lie down together;
>> and the lion shall eat straw like the ox.

One day the lion's friends asked how he could stand it, just lying there peacefully beside the lamb day in and day out, all the time. "Oh it's easy," replied the hungry lion. "It's a different lamb every day."

I often think of this joke when I reflect on the use and abuse of the idea of Christian friendship today. The short-term mission trip, with lots of photos of smiling "friends" that one never sees again; the cross-cultural summer internship spent living with a caring host family in a poor neighborhood—participating in such "friendship opportunities" is now essential to building up one's résumé in a globalizing world. Cross-cultural friendship opportunities emphasize the fun and the attraction of exploring new places, meeting new people, and learning across differences. The well-meaning friendship project sometimes ends up cultivating "a different lamb every day."

Contemporary studies of spirituality find a great longing for friendship on the part of ministry leaders, millennials, and others interested in meeting new people. As a middle-class citizen of the United States, it is especially important to ask some hard questions about the laudable desire to "make friends" with the poor, with migrants, and with others we meet around the world. As the stories in this book have shown, cross-cultural friendship does not take place in isolation. The path of friendship is shaped by its context—both the socio-politico-economic realities of the day and the particular characteristics of the friends themselves. Friendship may mean something quite different to an unemployed worker in an English slum in the year 1800 than to a Chinese Christian during the Cold War in the 1950s. It may mean something different to a South African woman and a Jamaican man, even if they are both living in London today. Even if friends are fellow followers of Christ, their definitions of friendship are influenced by differences in culture, differences in generation, and even generational differences within the same culture.

So what is the meaning of Christian friendship for those from the powerful American empire of endless war and huge military budgets? How do American churches move beyond lip service and actually embrace diverse friendships in an era of immigration restrictions, racial injustice, opioid deaths, and mass shootings committed by American citizens? Does friendship matter when the world is facing the destruction of ancient communities in Syria and Iraq, and global climate change? What is cross-cultural friendship when the denominations that produced the missionaries mentioned in this book are dividing along geographic lines and splitting over issues of gender and sexuality? American citizens, especially, need to approach cross-cultural friendships with a clear picture of its limitations—and their own. Similar to European imperialists a century ago, it is very easy for North Americans to act like the hungry lion enjoying a "different lamb every day."

A Bottom-Up Spiritual Practice, Not a Top-Down Strategy

The first limitation of friendship to mention is that it is a bottom-up spiritual practice, not a top-down formula for evangelization or structural change. Friendship involves individual persons, with all their unique needs and desires. Rudy Rasmus's "success" notwithstanding, it is not a strategy for social change enacted by religious professionals such as clergy and megachurch pastors. Neither is it a plan for systematic evangelization. Theologian Robert Schreiter, when writing about reconciliation a few years ago, concluded that it is a spirituality, not a strategy.[3] The same thing can be said about friendship as a Christian practice. Churches cannot plan "friendship campaigns" or "friendship projects," as if friendship can be neatly packaged into a set of steps. Friendship may grow organically from such "projects" as short-term mission trips or outreach to migrants or putting away the cell phone and greeting the lonely elderly. But it is very personal, requires investment of the whole self, and must go the distance. Embracing diversity through friendship is not an "efficient" plan of action.[4]

Friendship means following Jesus Christ in relation to others. Cost-benefit analyses of friendship would find it to be very expensive. Yet when you ask people who have lived in another culture in a spirit of Christian service what is the most important aspect of their experience, they typically say it is their close relationships with the friends they have made. When Philip Fugh and John Leighton Stuart became friends, little did they know that their family relationship would last beyond the grave, into the next generation. When Savarirayan Jesudason and Ernest Forrester-Paton started their pilgrimage together, it took the rest of their lives. When the Monday night group during the 1970s spent their time comforting the widows of unjustly executed Korean men and caring for the families of the imprisoned, they did it because they cared about the people, and their Christian values demanded it. They did not go into Korea with a friendship strategy—five friends today, ten friends in a month, a hundred friends in a year, and so forth. To truly befriend another person involves the unexpected, and it can take a lifetime.

Friendship with Jesus demands love of the neighbor, and considering her an equal. To be rooted in Jesus Christ, to "abide in the vine" (see John 15), is a spiritual practice, not a game plan. It begins at the bottom, at the level of basic human need for love, for relationships, and for God. It is not a plan for systematic change. It may feed profound fellowship, such as was experienced by Dr. Yu Enmei, missionary Dorothy McCammon, and other Christians in China during the Cold War.

Together in community, friends may recognize each other through attacking social injustices. Friendship may lead to persons following Jesus Christ. But the "purpose" of friendship spirituality is to honor the full humanity of the other as a fellow child of God.

The Problem of Power: Humility and Partnership

In most superhero stories, including the popular Marvel Studios movies, there is an orgy of violence. There are also profound stories of friendship. The movie *Captain America: The Winter Soldier* is no exception. Toward the end, Captain America realizes that the enemy he is called to fight is actually his old best friend, Bucky Barnes, whom he thought had died in the Second World War. Through brainwashing, Bucky had been transformed into the Winter Soldier, an assassin for evil forces. The moment of reckoning comes when Captain America and the Winter Soldier face each other. Insisting that the assassin's true name is Bucky, Captain America drops his shield and declares, "I'm not going to fight you. You're my friend." The Winter Soldier, aka Bucky, proceeds to beat Captain America to within an inch of his life. But when an explosion throws his old friend's body free, the Winter Soldier drags the unconscious Captain America to safety before disappearing into the woods.

While the fictional Captain America is not an emblem of Christian friendship, his decision not to fight Bucky says something important about the relationship between friendship and power. Captain America knows that to be a true friend to Bucky, he cannot use his superpowers against him. He risks letting Bucky kill him, and that is what nearly happens. Humility and loss of power are preconditions for re-awakening friendship with Bucky. And indeed, the posture of humility also changes the Winter Soldier enough to where he rescues his old friend—after having almost killed him first. Relinquishment of power is a precondition for friendship on both their parts.

For citizens of the contemporary American empire, humility and self-emptying are preconditions for friendship with persons of other cultures and religions. The income disparities between rich and poor nations and the global power wielded by the United States require self-criticism on the part of Americans if they wish to be friends with the poor or with persons from other nations. For privileged, middle-class, white North Americans, listening to others is the starting point. Instead of being driven by concrete project goals, Americans need to learn to spend time with, worship with, and enjoy life with international partners. As Frank Laubach learned from hard experience, seeking to "help" the Moros was not enough. He had to repent of his cultural arrogance, spend time with them, respect them, befriend them, and celebrate life with them. The dialogue of life cultivates friendship more than the dialogue of words.

The extent to which Americans should challenge the unjust systems as part of being friends with others is a difficult and personal question. While personal friendship involves solidarity with others, it is not about challenging structures per se. Nevertheless, history shows many situations in which caring about each other draws friends into the social and political struggles of their day. For example, Inus Daneel and Matteo Forridge defied the apartheid state through their cross-racial friendship during the Zimbabwean civil war. Caroline Macdonald and her allies sought prison reform in Japan. Savarirayan Jesudason and Ernest Forrester-Paton resisted British imperialism in India. Spencer Perkins and Chris Rice embodied interracial community in the segregated South. Through his love for Adam, Henri Nouwen became an advocate for the disabled.

In addition to requiring humility, cross-cultural Christian friendship today must operate in a larger framework of partnership with rather than power over others. After the Second World War, formal European colonialism was gradually dismantled. During this time of transition, there was a collapse of mission relationships that had been built during many decades of colonialism. Understandable yet painful transition in worldwide Christian community led to new structures for mission. Partnership began replacing paternalism. Instead of Western missionaries, activists, and donors calling the shots, it became essential that indigenous church leaders determine their own priorities. By the late 1960s, economic inequality, and the power that came with it, was becoming a front-burner issue in the effort to eliminate colonialism in cross-cultural relationships. Paternalism and Western control were directly connected to Western money. Missionaries who controlled donations from the West also set mission priorities. James Scherer's 1964 book, *Missionary, Go Home!* captured the mood about how Western domination, including financial resources, was stifling indigenous initiative.[5]

Over the past half century, the world church has grown in Africa, Asia, and Latin America. Many Western churches have lost vitality, and decline in membership characterizes much of Europe. In the context of the "shift southward,"[6] the urgency of partnership has only become stronger. Now there are networks of churches in Asia, Africa, and Latin America that have no memory of foreign leadership at all. Global migration means that church leaders in one country may have originated elsewhere. For example, many Nigerian pastors are now serving in Europe. Vietnamese Catholic priests are working in the United States. Instant communication through the internet allows leaders to network from around the world. Responsible cross-cultural relationships among churches worldwide assume the equality of partnership. Although there are many flaws in actual practice, in theory, the ideals of partnership characterize a world church in which compassionate mission flows from all directions to all directions.

Unlike in the 1920s, today "world friendship" among churches cannot be a formal movement brokered by Western missionaries. Rather, it needs to emerge through global relational networks such as the World Council of Churches, the Lausanne Movement, INFEMIT (International Fellowship of Mission as Transformation), the Global Christian Forum, and worldwide denominational groups—as well as through webs of personal relationships cultivated over time and place. The larger context of partnership, with practices of personal humility, should frame cross-cultural friendship today. For North Americans, becoming a friend with someone from another culture may involve less *doing for* and more *being with*. Being fully present with and for others requires listening in love and celebrating life together.

Cultural Respect

Cultural differences are one of the biggest challenges for faithful friendship. The classical view of friendship insisted that friends had to be equals and share cultures, social location, gender, and status in order to be true friends. In this book, I have argued that Jesus's writings and practices on friendship open up new possibilities based on common friendship with him. "What a friend we have in Jesus" opens the door to friendship between people who initially do not seem to have much in common. Caroline Macdonald and Tokichi Ishii, Henri Nouwen and Adam Arnett—there were profound differences of ethnicity, power, social class, and ability between them. Over time, however, the process of becoming friends involved discovering ways in which they were alike, while appreciating the unique gifts bestowed by their individuality and diversity.

Cultural respect is a precondition for cross-cultural friendship. It is impossible to see one's own culture from within. It is like the air we breathe—we do not notice it until we miss it. Embracing diversity reveals new dimensions of the human experience, as well as shining light on one's own limitations. Chris Rice and Spencer Perkins talked about "racial blinders," the ways in which one's racial affiliation limits one's perceptions of what life is like for someone of another race. Taking off racial blinders requires listening to the pain of someone from the other race without becoming defensive. Cultural blinders act the same way. Deliberate cultivation of respect for others is very important for those entering cross-cultural or interracial friendships. This respect requires listening, empathizing, and accepting without controlling the terms of the relationship.

Notice that I have stopped short of saying that "cultural competence" is a prerequisite for friendship. Under this framework, many organizations work hard to train students or employees in cultural sensitivity and to critique the unequal power and privileges that occur between persons of different classes, races, genders, gender identities, and cultures. Another helpful way to identify the challenges of cross-cultural relationships is through developing what missiologist David Livermore calls "cultural intelligence."[7] Yet in studying friendship, I see that mastery of another culture is not possible for most people. All friendships have blockages and limitations. For persons from different nations and ethnicities, cultural difference is a big challenge that can never be entirely overcome. Neither is the critical apparatus of cultural competence readily available for most people who are out there in real time making friends. Sometimes friendship is a matter of being a "holy fool," and rushing in where angels fear to tread. Friends share a mystery of belonging and a love of Christ that can transcend their differences. And as Savarirayan Jesudason noted, forgiveness is key to its success. Pursuing cultural competence and cultural intelligence are important goals. Yet faithful friendships are formed, and they persist despite the obstacles of cultural difference. Growth in grace toward the "other" is a lifetime process.

The problem of friendship and difference reminds me of an old joke from Maine. A family has lived in rural Maine for thirty years but still does not feel entirely welcome by the locals. The father of the family asks an elderly Mainer why, after so many years in Maine, he and his family are still considered outsiders. "Well now," replies the old Mainer, "if a cat crawled into the oven and had kittens, you wouldn't call them biscuits, would you?" This joke brings to mind what old-time missionaries called the problem of "cultural identification." No matter how much the missionary tried to identify with the local culture—learning the language, eating the food, dressing like a local, and accepting as much of the local culture as humanly possible—he or she was still usually seen as an outsider.[8]

One of the areas of difference that makes cross-cultural friendship especially difficult is that of gender. I have heard stories from multiple women who have been frustrated in their attempts to be friends with men of other cultures, or even to be treated as partners within church structures. Women are often stymied in their ability to be seen as equals in cross-cultural encounters. In many societies, the primary relationship permitted between adult men and women (besides blood relations) is that of sexual partners, ranging from marriage to prostitution. The chief example of male-female friendship mentioned in this book, that of Merrell Vories and Makiko Hitotsuyanagi, took place in the context of marriage; partnership in ministry had to be nested inside the socially acceptable relationship of marriage—and even their marriage was opposed because of their different ethnicities and social classes.

Culturally based understandings of gender roles are one of the toughest obstacles to navigate in crafting friendship across cultures. Most Americans are ignorant of how culture shapes gender relations. From the days of the early church, religious women have had to forgo physical relationships in order to be seen as gender neutral and therefore more able to enter into friendships with men. Gender neutrality has often been required for friendships to avoid the traditional cultural expectations attached to prescribed gender roles.[9] Celibacy has thus sometimes been a choice by persons seeking cross-cultural friendships.

Many of the friendships profiled in this book are between what might be called "third culture" people. These are folks who have immersed themselves in another culture and who share a cosmopolitan outlook that both appreciates and transcends cultural differences. The feeling that one's identity is caught between cultures is shared among third-culture people who sense they have more in common with each other than with people who are firmly ensconced in one particular culture. Third-culture people tend to be educated elites who travel and know people from other groups, and their numbers are growing in today's globalized world. Migration, education, and urbanization are big factors in the increasing numbers of people who can more readily pursue meaningful relationships with diverse people today.

Cultural respect is necessary for friendship. But while friendship requires serious attention to cultural differences, it does not depend on completely mastering another culture or on giving up one's own. Friends celebrate each other's differences. The process of friendship over time involves gradual learning about and appreciating the culture of the other person. People grow from differences shared with friends. The vision of the heavenly kingdom foretold in the book of Revelation is not one of boring sameness but of people from all races and nations worshipping and praising God together.

Friendship and Hope

If history is any indicator, we can be sure that right now, transformational, bridge-building friendships are taking place. We may not see them, but they are surely there—mustard seeds of hope for the future of Christian community and human solidarity.

Let me conclude this book by giving three brief examples of boundary-crossing Christian friendship today. These examples do not resolve all the challenges of befriending people unlike oneself. But the beauty of narrative is that life stories do not have to resolve anything. They just are. Their meaning is that they exist. Their very existence witnesses to hope for humanity.

In the age of controversy over immigration, Christians around the country are befriending undocumented immigrants at risk of deportation. Miriam Adeney, professor of world mission at Seattle Pacific University, tells the story of a group of undocumented Chinese immigrants who in the year 2000 smuggled themselves into the United States in shipping containers. Conditions on shipboard, trapped in the containers with limited food and water, were dire. Many died. When dock workers opened the containers in Seattle, out tumbled the rotten bodies. But thirty-four men were still alive. The US government put the men into a prisonlike detention center in the Pacific Northwest.[10] Their sufferings were immense.

Friendless and lonely, people could be imprisoned there for years while they waited for their cases to be adjudicated. Just like the poor locked away in debtors' prisons during the time of John Wesley, the friendless Chinese prisoners had no hope. The words of Jesus, which served as the motto of the Strangers' Friends Societies, come to mind: "I was an hungred, and ye gave me meat: I was a stranger, and ye took me in: naked, and ye clothed me: I was sick, and ye visited me" (Matt. 25:35–36, KJV). The detainees had no possessions and no ability to communicate in English or to represent themselves in the United States legal system.

As they awaited deportation, the undocumented Chinese were visited in prison by local Chinese Christians who brought them food and personal items like toothbrushes and clothing. The Chinese Americans visited them regularly and helped them navigate the American legal system over the months they were imprisoned. A relational network spread. Although the Chinese were deported in the end, they had become Christians in response to the friendship shown to them in their time of need. These "container Christians" witnessed to the good news while in prison. People from many different ethnic backgrounds came to Christ because of their testimony. Deported to China, they carried their witness back to their home country.

The witness of the Chinese detainees, who are now part of a relational global network, helps explain why Christianity is spreading as a world religion. Adeney points out that Christians working with the undocumented in the United States will often notify churches in the home countries of new converts so that after they are deported, they can be met at the airport by fellow believers—their new friends.

But the goal of friendship is not conversion, even though conversion may take place. Even in difficult circumstances with no apparent chance of "results," friendship remains a Christian calling. And so it was with Kayla Mueller, a Christian from Prescott, Arizona, who responded to the suffering of Syrians by volunteering among civil war refugees in 2012. In 2013, she volunteered with Doctors without Borders, a nonsectarian humanitarian organization that provides medical care in war zones, to refugees, and in other crisis situations. On August 4, Kayla and three others were captured by ISIS. While the other three were soon released, Kayla was accused of being an American spy. Thus began eighteen months of hell. She was kept as a personal slave by the notorious Abu Sayyaf and his abusive wife, who also arranged sex slaves for ISIS leadership. Moved from place to place to evade capture and seldom seen by other Western hostages, Kayla was repeatedly raped by the head of ISIS, Abu Bakr al-Baghdadi. During Kayla's time in captivity, the war with ISIS escalated. ISIS began publicly executing male hostages, and Western forces bombed their strongholds. As Kayla was a personal prisoner and an American citizen, ISIS refused to release her. In February 2015, at age twenty-six, she died. ISIS claimed she died when bombs were dropped by Jordan, but the American and Jordanian governments claim otherwise. Later, the wife of Abu Sayyaf was charged with her murder.

After Kayla's death, the story of her captivity was shared by others who had encountered her during their own captivities. They described a person of strong faith who cared for others despite the special abuse she endured. One hostage even described her defending her Christian faith to "Jihadi

John," a British ISIS executioner. But what other women captives remembered about Kayla was her friendship. One fellow prisoner from Doctors without Borders said, "As a person, she was a very good friend. She was smart. She was fun to be with. She was very kind, extremely generous. And she never stopped caring for others." For example, she tried to protect two young teenage Yazidi girls who were captured as sex slaves. As a religious minority considered heretical to Islam, the Yazidis were targeted for genocide by ISIS. The girls considered Kayla, ten years older, an older sister. She prayed for them to escape and survive. One of them, who wears a bracelet in Kayla's honor, later said in an interview, "She was very good to us. I will never forget."[11]

The friendship of Kayla Mueller with the other female captives was not an issue of religious conversion. It was a matter of being, an end in itself. And yet it was also a Christian witness, especially coming from an American woman who lacked political power. In fact, that she was an American caused her to be interrogated and humiliated all the more. She was treated as a personal representative of the enemy. Unlike the fictional Captain America, however, she did not survive the brutality of the Winter Soldier. Kayla prayed with and for the other women. Her Christian faith shone through in her fortitude and care for others. And the former captives remember her and testify to her faith and friendship.

A third example of Christian friendship today is that of Daryl Davis, an African American jazz pianist and devout Christian who befriends members of the Ku Klux Klan. He started down this surprising path when he began asking Klansmen, "Why do you hate me when you don't even know me?" Over the years, he has persuaded two hundred members of the Klan to leave the racist organization.

The documentary *Accidental Courtesy* traces Davis's beginnings to a childhood spent abroad, when his father was in the foreign service.[12] Davis grew up as a third-culture kid in interracial schools and settings. It was not until he moved back to the United States and joined the Cub Scouts that he experienced the realities of racism. He joined an all-white Scout troop in Belmont, Massachusetts. When he was carrying the American flag during a Scout parade, people began throwing bottles and rocks at him. Although the white Scout leaders moved in to protect him, when he got home, his parents explained to him that people attacked him because of the color of his skin.

Davis graduated from Howard University with a degree in jazz music. By 1983, he had joined a country music band. Music was the universal language that allowed Davis to start making personal connections with racists. He began meeting the clientele, some of whom were Klansmen. He undertook extended conversations that, over years, grew into friendships and invitations into each other's homes. Part of Davis's philosophy is that when people are talking together, even if they're pounding the table and shouting, they are communicating rather than fighting. Thus the beginning of friendship is to listen to others' points of view, even if you vehemently disagree with them. Find points of agreement, even about other subjects, and grow from there. Davis says that when Klansmen started to ask him questions as if his opinion mattered to them, he knew a turning point had been reached in their relationship.

Davis's Christian faith is important to how he approaches friendships with racists. One Klan family, the Puigs, were suffering because the father was in prison. Davis began driving the wife and kids to visit their loved one. Over time, the Puigs noticed that Davis was acting like more of a Christian than their fellow Klansmen were because he was helping them. They renounced racism and left the group. KKK Grand Dragon Roger Kelly became Davis's friend through a process of mutual listening and the frank exchange of views. After several years, Kelly left the Klan and gave Davis his pointed hood and white robe—the beginning of a collection of former Klansmen's robes. Davis was the godfather at the baptism of Kelly's daughter. One Klan organization, the Traditionalist American Knights, gave Davis a "Certificate of Friendship" for his friendship with its leaders over the years—even though the main leader did not leave the group. Discussions of biblical interpretation clearly had a role to play in Davis's engagement with the Traditionalist American Knights. His testimony to human equality under God was a convincing point of contact for Klansmen who claimed to be Christians.

One of the most interesting scenes in the documentary about Davis's life is when he has discussions with several younger African American activists, fresh from the rash of police killings of unarmed African Americans that sparked the Black Lives Matter movement. The younger men accuse Davis, who was born in 1958, of wasting his time on uplifting a few white people when he could be helping African Americans improve their lives. They did not believe white people could change. They derided his friendships with Klansmen, cursed him out, and walked out of the meeting, refusing to shake his hand.

Davis's response to this rejection of his perspective was to comment that people who make friends with people of other races are typically accused of being sellouts. Cross-racial and cross-cultural friendship has often meant being caught between opposing groups and being trusted by neither. Davis, however, believes "it is possible that change can occur."[13] As in Davis's case and those of others recounted in this chapter, friendship does not eliminate racism, ethnocentrism, and other injustices. And it is not a substitute for political action or structural change.

An inspiring part of Daryl Davis's life story is how the shared power of friendship changes all the people involved— the friends themselves, their families, and those to whom their friendship becomes a witness. Davis muses that he likes to tell his story because others are moved by it, and they tell even more people. "I never set out to convert anybody," he insists. When he first opened up dialogue by asking Klansmen why they hated him but didn't know him personally, they had no answers. In the end, "they ended up converting themselves."[14] The transformational mutuality of friendship across racial boundaries is apparent in Davis's summary remarks near the end of the film: "I have seen things change. I have seen people change. . . . I've changed."[15]

The three contemporary stories that conclude this book all show the transformative potential of Christian friendship. But the definitions of, paths to, and results of friendship are quite different. These stories exhibit the limitations and strengths of friendship that have characterized its theory and practices through the centuries. In them we see friendship through weakness and self-emptying humility—friendship "from the margins" of undocumented immigration, gender vulnerability, and racial prejudice. We see that friendship takes time, patience, self-control, and cheerfulness. Conversion to Christianity can be the result, or conversion to equal respect within Christianity, or no conversion except to friendship itself. The mutual vulnerability of friendship can also draw people toward other religions or into practices of multiple religious belonging.[16] Personal friendships are bottom-up practices, proceeding from person to person rather than top down. Contemporary boundary-crossing friendship is not a neat, packaged solution to the problems of church and world. But following in the way of Jesus Christ and many believers through the ages, it witnesses to the possibility of human flourishing.

Conclusion: Friendship on the Road

This book on Christian friendship started with Jesus and the disciples. It ends on the road, for the story of Christian friendship is not finished. It continues, though now in the hopeful light of the resurrection.

After Jesus's crucifixion and resurrection, the Gospel of Luke recounts that two of Jesus's disciples were walking from Jerusalem to the town of Emmaus. They conversed about the surprise of the empty tomb and the testimony of women who claimed he was alive. They speculated about what might have happened. They fell into conversation with a stranger about the meaning of the recent events. The stranger was very knowledgeable about religious matters, especially about prophecies regarding the Messiah. So they invited him to remain with them. Clearly they were enjoying the conversation. As he blessed the bread for their supper, they realized that the stranger was in fact the risen Jesus himself. He disappeared, and they raced back to tell the others they had seen the Lord. As they told their story, it spread to others, who shared it again—links in the chain of salvation history through the ages.

The walk to Emmaus was a pilgrimage of friendship. It involved greater self- knowledge of the disciples' identity in relation to each other in light of the risen Jesus. The pilgrims headed together toward shelter, conversing along the way. They did not understand everything they encountered, but they grew together on their common path. As they enjoyed their fellowship, Jesus was revealed to them in the breaking of bread. Eating with a stranger, embracing relationships across boundaries, was how God became known to them. Fellowship on the road turned strangers into friends and made Christian community possible.

APPENDIX

Notes on the Challenges of Narrating Friendship

For those who are not interested in the academic challenges of writing this book, I invite them to skip this section. But for those who wish to read about my scholarly assumptions and limitations, feel free to keep reading.

Reflection on the history and practice of cross-cultural friendship is full of challenges. The first problem is that of white Western expansionism through history. Ample scholarship on colonialism and Western mission from the 1400s to the 1900s paints an often dismal picture of mission as the handmaiden of racist expansionism by Westerners unwilling to treat other people as equals. Without contradicting that scholarly framework, this book nevertheless recounts a counter narrative in which Christians have done their best, through specific cross-cultural friendships, to reject oppressive imperialistic structures and racial prejudices. Faithful friendships represent an alternative set of practices without which Christianity could never have become a worldwide community of faith.

A second challenge in narrating cross-cultural friendship is the nature of friendship itself. Friendship is mutual. It is not coercive. It goes in both directions and commits to sacrificial relationship. In many cultures, it carries lifelong obligations. To analyze cross-cultural friendship in the context of building Christian community risks turning friendship into a "strategy" that manipulates other people. So-called friendship that is quantified or strategized loses its authenticity. Although cross-cultural friendship may be mutually beneficial for multiple purposes, it is not a calculated means to power over another person. At the same time, friendship is powerful in its potential for transformation.

Third, as postcolonialist scholar Gayatri Spivak asked so clearly some years ago, "Can the subaltern speak?"[1] In other words, in a world of inequality, with historical evidence and scholarly reflection mediated largely through the framework of the privileged—usually white Westerners—can we ever truly hear the voices of the disadvantaged who are being spoken for? Is it possible to hear the voices of the poor, of women and children, and of the victims of injustice when the only access we have to their realities is through the perspective of others more powerful than they? Most of the stories recounted in this book are subject to this limitation in that they have been written in English and compiled by literate Westerners. Then they are being analyzed again by me, a white, middle-class scholar, with the limitations that my privileged status confers. And yet, I assert that in the very existence of shared relationships, multiple voices can be heard, even if some voices are louder than others.

Discerning readers will also note that my case studies do not include many examples of friendship between women.

This, too, stems from a problem of documentation. Women often experience the church as a primary friendship network, and feminist and womanist theologians often point out that relationality characterizes women's approach to God, theology, and Christian practices. Nevertheless, biographies and other written sources heavily favor male voices, with the possible exception of women who have written about their relationships with their husbands. The recovery of women's voices on particular cross-cultural friendships remains a challenge to carry forward in further research. Ironically, perhaps because friendship between women is seen as so ordinary, it is less documented than exemplary friendships between men.

Finally, studying friendships is uniquely difficult because it involves delving into the details of personal biography, looking for things people typically take for granted and therefore do not document. For over thirty years, I have been teaching mission studies and researching world Christianity. I have read a multitude of books and articles on evangelization, social justice, and theologies of mission. I have read hundreds of historical and theological critiques of Christianity as dependent on the evils of Western colonialism. I have studied conference reports, minutes from mission meetings, and handbooks and encyclopedias about mission, but I seldom see close historical analysis of the relationship between specific friendships and Christian community. Why is this? Perhaps because friendship is personal and relational. Because it is typically not documented in written sources, it flies under the radar as an invisible factor in theory and practice.

NOTES

ACKNOWLEDGMENTS

1. In 2010, I delivered the Henry Drummond Lecture in Stirling, Scotland, subsequently published as Dana L. Robert, "Cross-Cultural Friendship in the Creation of Twentieth-Century World Christianity," *International Bulletin of Missionary Research* 35, no. 2 (April 1, 2011): 100–107. The Augsburger Lectures at Eastern Mennonite University were condensed and published as Dana L. Robert, "Global Friendship as Incarnational Missional Practice," *International Bulletin of Missionary Research* 39, no. 4 (October 1, 2015): 180–84.

INTRODUCTION

1. Stephen Marche, "Is Facebook Making Us Lonely?" *The Atlantic* (May 2012), https://www.theatlantic.com/magazine/archive/2012/05/is-facebook -making-us-lonely/308930/.
2. Marche, "Is Facebook Making Us Lonely?"
3. Hugh Black, *Friendship* (Chicago: Fleming H. Revell, 1898), 55.
4. John Donne, "Meditation XVII," in *Devotions upon Emergent Occasions* (London, 1624).
5. All Scripture references, unless otherwise noted, use the New Revised Standard Version.
6. James H. Kroeger, ed., *The Gift of Mission: Yesterday, Today, Tomorrow: The Maryknoll Centennial Symposium* (Maryknoll, NY: Orbis Books, 2013).

7. In 1973, Orbis Books, the imprint of the Maryknoll Fathers and Brothers, first published Father Gustavo's influential book *A Theology of Liberation*. See Gustavo Gutiérrez, *A Theology of Liberation: History, Politics, and Salvation*, rev. ed. (Maryknoll, NY: Orbis Books, 1988).

8. One implication of using historical texts from the twentieth century is that male language for God and humanity predominates. I have not attempted to change or update gender categories when quoting people. I have kept their words as they wrote them.

9. For the idea of indwelling the Scripture narrative, see Lesslie Newbigin, *Foolishness to the Greeks: The Gospel and Western Culture* (Grand Rapids: Eerdmans, 1988).

10. By *Christian practice*, I mean "things Christian people do together over time to address fundamental human needs in response to and in the light of God's active presence for the life of the world," a definition taken from Craig Dykstra and Dorothy C. Bass, "A Theological Understanding of Christian Practices," in *Practicing Theology: Beliefs and Practices in Christian Life*, ed. Miroslav Volf and Dorothy C. Bass (Grand Rapids: Eerdmans, 2002), 18.

11. The subject of "culture" is huge, with important literature generated by the social sciences and humanities. For the purpose of this book, I am using a simple definition from the *Oxford English Dictionary* (definition 7a). Culture is "the distinctive ideas, customs, social behaviour, products, or way of life of a particular nation, society, people, or period. Hence: a society or group characterized by such customs, etc." http://www.oed.com/view/Entry/45746?rskey=4MRgi8&result=1#eid.

12. Emmanuel M. Katongole, *Mirror to the Church: Resurrecting Faith after Genocide in Rwanda* (Grand Rapids: Zondervan, 2009), 156. The Rwandan genocide occurred when one group of Rwandan Christians murdered those seen as the ethnic "other."

CHAPTER 1

1. Robert D. Schildgen, *Toyohiko Kagawa: An Apostle of Love and Social Justice* (Berkeley: Centenary Books, 1988), 133.

2. Elias Chacour with David Hazard, *Blood Brothers: The Dramatic Story of a Palestinian Christian Working for Peace in Israel* (Grand Rapids: Baker Books, 2013), 63.

3. My reflections are based on an amateur's reading of the text. The Latin origin of the word *amateur* is *amator*, lover. My use of the term comes from my Swiss Protestant ancestors of the 1530s—early Protestants known as "amateurs de l'Evangile," lovers of the gospel.

4. Willard M. Swartley, *John: Believers Church Bible Commentary* (Harrisonburg, VA: Herald Press, 2013).

5. Stanley H. Skreslet, *Picturing Christian Witness: New Testament Images of Disciples in Mission* (Grand Rapids: Eerdmans, 2006).

6. Donald McGavran, *Bridges of God: A Study in the Strategy of Missions* (Eugene, OR: Wipf & Stock, 2005).

7. Alan Kreider and Eleanor Kreider, *Worship and Mission after Christendom* (Harrisonburg, VA: Herald Press, 2011), 223–24.

8. Hans Hübner, "menō," in *Exegetical Dictionary of the New Testament*, vol. 2, ed. Horst Balz and Gerhard Schneider (Grand Rapids: Eerdmans, 1991), 407.

9. Andrew Murray, *Abide in Christ* (New Kensington, PA: Whitaker House, 2002); Henri J. M. Nouwen, *Lifesigns: Intimacy, Fecundity, and Ecstasy in Christian Perspective* (New York: Image/Doubleday, 1989).

10. Dana L. Robert, *Joy to the World! Mission in the Age of Global Christianity* (New York: Women's Division, General Board of Global Ministries, United Methodist Church, 2010), 47.

11. Samuel E. Escobar, *Changing Tides: Latin America and World Mission Today* (Maryknoll, NY: Orbis Books, 2002).

12. Kosuke Koyama, *Water Buffalo Theology* (Maryknoll, NY: Orbis Books, 1999), 66.

13. This story is recounted in Robert, *Joy to the World!*, 109–11. It occurred about a decade before the Black Lives Matter movement.

14. Lyndle Bullard, quoted in Joel Wendland, "Jena Six Case Exposes Right-wing Media Double Standard," http://politicalaffairs.net, September 24–30, 2007.

15. Lyndle Bullard, quoted in Abbey Brown, "September 20, 2008: 'Jena Six' Rally, Spotlight Left Impact on Community," www.thetowntalk.com.

16. Brown, "September 20, 2008."

17. Jimmy Young, quoted in Brown, "September 20, 2008."

18. Joanne Doi, "Bridge to Compassion: Theological Pilgrimage to Tule Lake and Manzanar" (PhD diss., Graduate Theological Union, 2007), 219.

19. For example, see the classic by Anders Nygren, *Agape and Eros*, trans. Philip S. Watson (Philadelphia: Westminster, 1953).

20. C. S. Lewis, *The Four Loves* (New York: Harvest Books/Harcourt Brace Jovanovich, 1971), 84.

21. Lewis, *Four Loves*, 89. In this book, Lewis's treatment of friendship is problematic with regard to his treatment of gender. But his image of friends standing side by side, focusing on their common vision, remains helpful.

22. Lewis, *Four Loves*, 91.

CHAPTER 2

1. Constant J. Mews, "Cicero on Friendship," in *Friendship: A History*, ed. Barbara Caine (London: Routledge, 2009), 66.

2. Dirk Baltzly and Nick Eliopoulos, "The Classical Ideals of Friendship," in *Friendship: A History*, 43.

3. Constant J. Mews and Neville Chiavaroli, "The Latin West," in *Friendship: A History*, 79.

4. Mews and Chiavaroli, "The Latin West," 88–89.

5. David Garrioch, "From Christian Friendship to Secular Sentimentality: Enlightenment Re-evaluations," in *Friendship: A History*, 172.

6. Carolyn James and Bill Kent, "Renaissance Friendships: Traditional Truths, New and Dissenting Voices," in *Friendship: A History*, 111–64.

7. Ricci is only the most famous example of the friendship network that emerged between the Jesuits and Chinese Confucian scholars. According to Claudia von Collani, "A number of missionaries and Chinese literati became good friends. This is not astonishing, as both sides adhered to the same values, i.e., learning, high morals, education, philosophy, art and literature; both despised wealth and material matters, and both based, at least to a certain extent, their thinking and actions on reason." See Claudia von Collani, "Missionising from Inside: Lady Candida Xu: The Role of Chinese Women in Chinese Christianity," in *Europe in China, China in Europe: Mission as a Vehicle to Intercultural Dialogue—Lectures of the Symposium for the 400th Anniversary of Matteo Ricci (1552–1610), Zurich University, June 14th–15th, 2010* (Stuttgart, Germany: Franz Steiner Verlag, 2012), 49.

8. On the importance of Ricci's friendship with Qu Rukuei and other literati, see Andrew C. Ross, *A Vision Betrayed: The Jesuits in Japan and China, 1542–1742* (Maryknoll, NY: Orbis Books, 2003), 124–26. Chinese usage typically puts the family name before the personal name, a practice I have largely followed in this book.

9. Christopher Shelke and Mariella Demichele, eds., *Matteo Ricci in China: Inculturation through Friendship and Faith* (Rome: Gregorian & Biblical Press, 2010).

10. Shelke and Demichele, *Matteo Ricci in China*, 47.

11. Matteo Ricci, "A Treatise on Friendship," in Shelke and Demichele, *Matteo Ricci in China*, 53.

12. Ricci, "Treatise on Friendship" 57.

13. Aloysius Jin Luxian, "In Praise of Xu Guangqi," *China Heritage Quarterly*, no. 23 (September 2010), http://www.chinaheritagequarterly.org/features.php?searchterm=023_guangqi.inc&issue=023.

14. "Xu Guangqi," *New World Encyclopedia*, http://www.newworldencyclopedia.org/entry/Xu_Guangqi.

15. Quoted in Luxian, "In Praise of Xu Guangqi."

16. For an overview of Xu's remarkable ministry, see Claudia von Collani, "Missionising from Inside: Lady Candida Xu: The Role of Chinese Women in Chinese Christianity," in *Europe in China, China in Europe*, 49–70. See also Gail King, "Candida Xu and the Growth of Christian-

ity in China in the Seventeenth Century," *Monumenta Serica* 46 (1998): 49–66.

17. Eugenio Menegon, *Ancestors, Virgins, and Friars: Christianity as a Local Religion in Late Imperial China* (Cambridge, MA: Harvard University Asia Center for the Harvard-Yenching Institute, 2009).

18. Tim Macquiban, "Friends of All? The Wesleyan Response to Urban Poverty in Britain and Ireland, 1785–1840," in *The Poor and the People Called Methodists*, ed. Richard P. Heizenrater (Nashville: Abingdon, 2002), 132.

19. Randy L. Maddox, *Responsible Grace: John Wesley's Practical Theology* (Nashville: Kingswood Books, 1994), 151.

20. *The Nature, Design, and Rules of the Benevolent, or Strangers' Friend Society* (London: J. Butterworth, 1809), 6.

21. Quoted in Steve Hindle, Alexandra Shepard, and John Walter, eds., *Remaking English Society* (Woodbridge: Boydell, 2015), 83.

22. See front of report in *Nature, Design, and Rules*.

23. *Nature, Design, and Rules*, 7, 46–60.

24. See, for example, Robert D. Lupton, *Toxic Charity: How Churches and Charities Hurt Those They Help, and How to Reverse It* (New York: HarperOne, 2012); Steve Corbett and Brian Fikkert, *When Helping Hurts: How to Alleviate Poverty without Hurting the Poor . . . and Yourself* (Chicago: Moody Publishers, 2014).

25. *Nature, Design, and Rules*, 16.

26. *Nature, Design, and Rules*, 17.

27. *Nature, Design, and Rules*, 40.

28. *Nature, Design, and Rules*, 40.

29. Maddox, *Responsible Grace*, 77.

30. John Wesley, quoted in Maddox, *Responsible Grace*, 78.

31. "Japanese-American Relations at the Turn of the Century, 1900–1922," Office of the Historian, United States Department of State, https://history.state.gov/milestones/1899-1913/japanese-relations.

32. Dana L. Robert, "Christian Transnationalists, Nationhood and the Construction of Civil Society," in *Religion and Innovation: Antagonists or Partners?*, ed. Donald A. Yerxa (Broadway, NY: Bloomsbury Academic, 2016), 144.

33. Michi Kawai, *My Lantern* (Tokyo: Kyo Bun Kwan, 1939); Sharon Yamato Danley, "Japanese Picture Brides Recall Hardships of American Life," *Los Angeles Times*, May 11, 1995.

34. Sidney L. Gulick, quoted in Sandra Taylor, *Advocate of Understanding: Sidney Gulick and the Search for Peace with Japan* (Kent, OH: Kent State University Press, 1985), 77.

35. Sidney L. Gulick, *The American Japanese Problem: A Study of the Racial Relations of the East and the West* (New York: Charles Scribner's, 1914).

36. Dana L. Robert, *American Women in Mission: The Modern Mission Era, 1792–1992* (Macon, GA: Mercer University Press, 1997), 273.

37. Mary Isham, *Valorous Ventures: A Record of Sixty and Six Years of the*

Woman's Foreign Missionary Society, Methodist Episcopal Church (Boston: Woman's Foreign Missionary Society, Methodist Episcopal Church, 1936), 85.

38. Robert, "Global Friendship," 180.

39. Taylor, *Advocate of Understanding,* 180.

40. Bill Gordon, "Japanese Friendship Dolls History," http://wgordon .web.wesleyan.edu/dolls/japanese/history/index.htm.

41. Ricci, "Treatise on Friendship," 57.

CHAPTER 3

1. Margaret Prang, *A Heart at Leisure from Itself: Caroline Macdonald of Japan* (Vancouver: UBC Press, 2002).

2. Brian Stanley, *The World Missionary Conference, Edinburgh 1910* (Grand Rapids: Eerdmans, 2009).

3. Robert D. Schildgen, *Toyohiko Kagawa: An Apostle of Love and Social Justice* (Berkeley: Centenary Books, 1988).

4. Prang, *Heart at Leisure,* 144–48.

5. Tokichi Ishii, *A Gentleman in Prison: With the Confessions of Tokichi Ishii Written in Tokyo Prison* (London: Forgotten Books, 2017).

6. Prang, *Heart at Leisure,* 147

7. Prang, *Heart at Leisure,* 147.

8. Caroline Macdonald, quoted in Prang, *Heart at Leisure,* 274.

9. Prang, *Heart at Leisure,* 294.

10. Caroline Macdonald, quoted in Prang, *Heart at Leisure,* 268.

11. Prang, *Heart at Leisure,* 273.

12. This section of the book about Jesudason and Forrester-Paton is modified from the manuscript of my book in progress, *The Transnational Imagination: Constructing World Christianity as a Political Force, 1889–1939* [working title].

13. Savarirayan Jesudason, *Reminiscences of a Pilgrim of Life: An Autobiography* (Vellore, Tamil Nadu: Sri Ramachandra Press, 1959), 60.

14. Ernest Forrester-Paton, *The Christukula Ashram (Family of Christ Ashram) at Tirupattur, N.A., South India* (Royapettah, Madras: N.M.S. Press, 1940), 5.

15. Jesudason, *Reminisces,* 74.

16. Forrester-Paton, *Christukula Ashram,* 5.

17. Richard Taylor points out that despite Jesudason's seniority as "older brother," Forrester-Paton's family wealth stabilized the ashram and paid for its buildings. Richard W. Taylor, "Christian Ashrams as a Style of Mission in India," *International Review of Mission* 68, no. 271 (July 1979): 287.

18. Traditionally, an ashram is a residential Hindu spiritual community gathered around a guru. When Christians began founding ashrams in the early twentieth century, they typically saw Jesus Christ as the head of their communities. Forrester-Paton writes, "The family at the Ashram is aimed

to be a fellowship of likeminded souls inspired by a common devotion to a common head Jesus Christ, and united to one another by personal love" (Forrester-Paton, *Christukula Ashram*, 25).

19. Jesudason, *Reminiscences*, 77. Forrester-Paton recalled that his mother's support for his friendship with Jesudason gave him great strength. She called Jesudason by the pet name Thamby and considered him "another son." Ernest Forrester-Paton, *Reminiscences of Early Years* (Tirupattur: Christu Kula Ashram Press, 1952), 70.

20. Forrester-Paton, *Christukula Ashram*, 47.

21. Forrester-Paton, *Christukula Ashram*, 35.

22. Forrester-Paton, *Christukula Ashram*, 48.

23. Forrester-Paton, *Christukula Ashram*, 50–51.

24. Forrester-Paton, *Christukula Ashram*, 73.

25. Forrester-Paton, *Christukula Ashram*, 59.

26. Jesudason, *Reminiscences*, 130.

27. Jesudason, *Reminiscences*, 130.

28. Sages of the New Covenant, http://www.ncsages.org/ccrd/christu-kula_Ashram_songs.

29. In later years, Andrews lived at the Christukula Ashram and supported its work. The ashram movement had the full support also of the famous missionary E. Stanley Jones, who attended the conference.

30. Kenneth G. Grubb and the International Missionary Council, eds., *The Church and the State: Presenting Papers Based upon the Meeting of the International Missionary Council, at Tambaram, Madras, India, December 12th to 29th, 1938* (New York: International Missionary Council, 1939).

31. Dorothy Snapp McCammon, *We Tried to Stay* (Harrisonburg, VA: Herald Press, 1953), 136.

32. McCammon, *We Tried to Stay*, 140.

33. McCammon, *We Tried to Stay*, 159.

34. F. Olin Stockwell, *With God in Red China: The Story of Two Years in Chinese Communist Prisons* (New York: Harper, 1953); F. Olin Stockwell, *Meditations from a Prison Cell: Devotional Talks from a Chinese Communist Prison* (Nashville: The Upper Room, 1954).

35. Dorothy Snapp McCammon, *Tragedy and Triumph: Courage and Faith through Twenty-Seven Years in Chinese Prisons—The Story of Dr. Yu Enmei as Told to Dorothy McCammon*, ed. Harriet Lapp Burkholder (San Francisco: Purple Bamboo, 1993).

36. McCammon clearly refers to Enmei by initial in *Tragedy and Triumph*, 121–23, when she mentions helping "E." at the clinic, and possibly on pages 197–98.

37. McCammon, *Tragedy and Triumph*, v.

38. Ruth Yu Hsaio, introduction to *Tragedy and Triumph*, xi.

39. Quoted in McCammon, *Tragedy and Triumph*, 71–72.

40. McCammon, *Tragedy and Triumph*, 61.

41. Quoted in McCammon, *Tragedy and Triumph*, 64.

42. McCammon, *Tragedy and Triumph*, 60.

43. Quoted in McCammon, *Tragedy and Triumph*, 95.

44. Quoted in McCammon, *Tragedy and Triumph*, 111.

45. Rom. 4:14; 1 Cor. 1:17, 9:15; 2 Cor. 9:3; Phil.2:7.

46. René Voillaume, *Seeds of the Desert: The Legacy of Charles de Foucauld* (London: Burns and Oates, 1955), 72.

47. Voillaume, *Seeds of the Desert*, 73–74.

48. Voillaume, *Seeds of the Desert*, 76. By the 1960s, the spirituality of Christian presence had spread widely through mission writings and the work of the Student Christian Movement. It had a big impact on the unfolding spirituality of "accompaniment" that emerged with the advent of liberation theology around 1970 in Latin America.

49. Christopher L. Heuertz and Christine D. Pohl, *Friendship at the Margins: Discovering Mutuality in Service and Mission* (Downers Grove, IL: InterVarsity Press, 2010), 28.

CHAPTER 4

1. Duncan Hamilton, *For the Glory: The Untold and Inspiring Story of Eric Liddell, Hero of Chariots of Fire* (New York: Penguin Books, 2017); David McCasland, *Eric Liddell: Pure Gold: The Olympic Champion Who Inspired Chariots of Fire* (Grand Rapids: Discovery House, 2001).

2. The idea of self-emptying for the sake of others, or *kenōsis*, comes from the idea that Jesus freely gave up his own will and privileged divinity to become human and to die upon the cross. Jesus's act of renunciation was celebrated in the early church through hymns and prayers—for example, Phil. 2:6–8.

3. "Vories' Architectural Legacy in Danger of Crumbling Away," *Japan Times*, February 6, 2006, http://www.japantimes.co.jp/news/2006/02/16/national/vories-architectural-legacy-in-danger-of-crumbling-away/. For the William Merrell Vories Library, devoted to his memory by the Omi Brotherhood Group, see http://vories.com/english/.

4. Grace Fletcher, *The Bridge of Love* (New York: E. P. Dutton, 1967), 65.

5. William Merrell Vories, *A Mustard-Seed in Japan* (Omihachiman: Omi Mission, 1925), 11; William Merrell Vories, *The Omi Brotherhood in Nippon: A Brief History of "the Omi Mission" Founded in Omi-Hachiman, Japan, in 1905* (Omihachiman: Omi Brotherhood, 1934), 11.

6. Vories, *Omi Brotherhood*, 11–12.

7. Vories, *Omi Brotherhood*, 16.

8. Vories, *Omi Brotherhood*, 141.

9. Vories, *Omi Brotherhood*, 77–82.

10. Vories, *Omi Brotherhood*, 103.

11. Vories, *Omi Brotherhood*, 109.

12. Vories sought to play famous organs whenever possible, including that of Riverside Church in New York City and the Saint-Saëns organ in Paris. See Fletcher, *Bridge of Love*, 139–41.

13. William Merrell Vories, *Goro Takagi, Musician: A Tribute* (Omihachiman: Omi Brotherhood, 1934), 50–51.

14. Vories, *Goro Takagi, Musician*, 50–51.

15. Vories, *Goro Takagi, Musician*, 72.

16. Vories, *Goro Takagi, Musician*, 68.

17. Vories, *Goro Takagi, Musician*, 70, 131.

18. Vories, *Goro Takagi, Musician*, 79.

19. Quoted in Fletcher, *Bridge of Love*, 146.

20. Quoted in Fletcher, *Bridge of Love*, 145.

21. Quoted in Fletcher, *Bridges of Love*, 158. Merrell and Maki remained in Japan through the war, as did Merrell's mother. During the United States' subsequent occupation of Japan under General Douglas MacArthur, Merrell played an informal role as go-between for the Japanese royal family and the American military. Merrell advised Emperor Hirohito to renounce his divinity.

22. Quoted in Garrioch, "From Christian Friendship," 175.

23. Vories, *Omi Brotherhood*, 120.

24. Gwen Terasaki and Mariko Terasaki Miller, *Bridge to the Sun: A Memoir of Love and War* (Casper, WY: Rock Creek Books, 2012).

25. On Alice Jay Kurusu, see Neal Henry Lawrence, "The Unforgettable Alice Kurusu, Wife of a Diplomat," *Asiatic Society of Japan*, May 5, 2000, http://www.asjapan.org/web.php/lectures/2000/05.

26. Mao Zedong, "Report on an Investigation of the Peasant Movement in Hunan," in *Selected Works of Mao Tse-tung*, vol. 1 (Peking: Foreign Languages Press, 1975), 23–29.

27. Dana L. Robert, "Cross-Cultural Friendship in the Creation of Twentieth-Century World Christianity," *International Bulletin of Missionary Research* 35, no. 2 (April 1, 2011): 100–107.

28. John Leighton Stuart, *Fifty Years in China: The Memoirs of John Leighton Stuart, Missionary and Ambassador* (New York: Random House, 1954), 124.

29. Stuart, *Fifty Years in China*, 289

30. Robert, "Cross-Cultural Friendship," 103.

31. On the life of Liu, see John Barwick, "Liu Tingfang: Christian Minister and Activist Intellectual," in *Salt and Light, Volume 3: More Lives of Faith That Shaped Modern China* (Eugene, OR: Wipf & Stock, 2011), 59–80.

32. Correspondence with Leighton Stuart, Missionary Research Library Archives, "Section 6: China," Timothy Tingfang Lew Papers, series 2, box 1, folder 17, Burke Library, Union Theological Seminary, Columbia University, New York.

33. Stuart to Liu, May 15, 1947, Lew Papers.

34. "Post-War Planning and the Chinese Church: A Preliminary Study of Some of the Essential Features," Lew Papers.

35. Mao Zedong, *Selected Works of Mao Tse-tung*, vol. 4 (Peking: Foreign Languages Press, 1969), 439.

36. Jane Leung Larson, "John L. Fugh and J. Stapleton Roy in Conversation: The Philip Fugh Family, Ambassador John Leighton Stuart, and U.S.-China Relations," Committee of 100, http://committee100.typepad.com/committee_of_100_newslett/2008/12/john-l-fugh-and-j-stapleton-roy-in-conversation-the-philip-fugh-family-ambassador-john-leighton-stua.html.

37. Unfortunately, Stuart was not allowed to be buried next to his wife, as that would have put him in the center of what is now Peking University. Yenching University was dismantled by the Communist government and its site given to Peking University.

38. Larson, "Fugh and Roy in Conversation."

39. "Obituary: Andrew Tod Roy/Missionary, Teacher in China," *Pittsburgh Post-Gazette*, May 6, 2004, http://www.post-gazette.com/news/obituaries/2004/05/07/Obituary-Andrew-Tod-Roy-Missionary-teacher-in-China/stories/200405070174.

40. For the story of the Thornberrys and Peng, see Milo L. Thornberry, *Fireproof Moth: A Missionary in Taiwan's White Terror* (Mechanicsburg, PA: Sunbury Press, 2011).

41. Dietrich Bonhoeffer, *Life Together: The Classic Exploration of Christian in Community* (New York: HarperOne, 2009), 20.

42. Bonhoeffer, *Life Together*, 21.

43. Bonhoeffer, *Life Together*, 25.

CHAPTER 5

1. Paul Halsall, "Rhodesia: Unilateral Declaration of Independence Documents, 1965," *Modern History Sourcebook*, July 1998, https://sourcebooks.fordham.edu/mod/1965Rhodesia-UDI.html.

2. African Independent Churches were defined by Harold Turner as churches founded by Africans, in Africa, for Africans. More recent nomenclature for these churches calls them African Indigenous Churches or African Initiated Churches.

3. David B. Barrett, *Schism and Renewal in Africa* (Oxford: Oxford University Press, 1968).

4. David A. Shank, "Mission Relations with the Independent Churches in Africa," *Missiology: An International Review* 13, no. 1 (1985): 42.

5. M. L. Daneel, *Fambidzano: Ecumenical Movement of Zimbabwean Independent Churches* (Gweru, Zimbabwe: Mambo Press, 1989). For photographs and

scanned publications by Daneel, see the website Old and New in Shona Religion, http://sites.bu.edu/shonareligion/.

6. For the story of this event, and how it culminated in Daneel's return to the pulpit several decades later, see Dana L. Robert, "Zimbabwe Testimony," *Focus* (Winter 2008–9): 49–52.

7. M. L. Daneel, interview by author, October 3, 2017.

8. Later confronted with Forridge's position as an AIC bishop, Dutch Reformed missionaries were surprised to find that their "postman" was such an important ecumenical leader.

9. When asked why AIC leaders protected him during the war, Daneel replied, "My loyalty was to the people. . . . The people accepted this and preached about my noninvolvement. I was theirs." Interview by author, October, 3, 2017.

10. Jim Stentzel, ed., *More Than Witnesses: How a Small Group of Missionaries Aided Korea's Democratic Revolution* (Mequon, WI: Nightengale Press, 2008).

11. Faye Moon, "Heartaches No Longer, and Some That Linger," in Stenzel, ed., *More Than Witnesses*, 148–49.

12. Marion Kim, "One Community across All Boundaries," in *More Than Witnesses*, 230.

13. Kim, *One Community*, 238–39.

14. Gene Mathews, "Things They Never Taught Us Down on the Farm," in *More than Witnesses*, 205.

15. Mathews, "Things They Never Taught Us," 214.

16. Mathews, "Things They Never Taught Us," 222.

17. "The Role of the Church in Facing the Nation's Chief Moral Dilemma," address delivered at the Conference on Christian Faith and Human Relations, Nashville, April 25, 1997, 190, http://okra.stanford.edu/tran scription/document_images/Vol04Scans/184_1957_The%20Role%20of%20 the%20Church.pdf.

18. Spencer Perkins and Chris Rice, *More Than Equals: Racial Healing for the Sake of the Gospel* (Downers Grove, IL: InterVarsity Press, 2000).

19. Perkins and Rice, *More Than Equals*, 98

20. John M. Perkins and Randy Alcorn, *Dream with Me: Race, Love, and the Struggle We Must Win* (Grand Rapids: Baker Books, 2017); John M. Perkins, *Beyond Charity: The Call to Christian Community Development* (Grand Rapids: Baker Books, 1993).

21. Perkins and Rice, *More Than Equals*, 58.

22. Perkins and Rice, *More Than Equals*, 208.

23. Perkins and Rice, *More Than Equals*, 209.

24. Perkins and Rice, *More Than Equals*, 210.

25. Quoted in Perkins and Rice, *More Than Equals*, 224.

26. Quoted in Perkins and Rice, *More Than Equals*, 189–90.

27. Perkins and Rice, *More Than Equals*, 231.

28. Perkins and Rice, *More Than Equals*, 242.

29. Jürgen Moltmann, "Wrestling with God: A Personal Meditation," *Christian Century* 114, no. 23 (August 13–20, 1997): 727.

30. John Wesley mentioned these words of Isaac Watts's in his obituary tribute to his brother, Charles, at the Methodist Conference in 1788. Quoted in *The United Methodist Hymnal: Book of United Methodist Worship* (Nashville: United Methodist Publishing House, 1989), 387.

CHAPTER 6

1. Edwin W. Smith, *The Golden Stool: Some Aspects of the Conflict of Cultures in Modern Africa* (London: Edinburgh House, 1926), 324–25. For Smith's leadership in reframing missionary perspectives on African traditional religions, see Edwin W. Smith, *The Christian Mission in Africa: A Study Based on the Work of the International Committee at LeZoute, Belgium, September 14th to 21st, 1926* (New York: International Missionary Council, 1926). This discussion of Smith is also found in Dana L. Robert, "Cross-Cultural Friendship in the Creation of Twentieth-Century World Christianity," *International Bulletin of Missionary Research* 35, no. 2 (April 1, 2011): 102.

2. Frank C. Laubach, *Letters by a Modern Mystic*, ed. Gina Brandon and Karen Friesen (Colorado Springs: Purposeful Design Publications, 2007), 59.

3. Laubach, *Letters by Modern Mystic*, 60.

4. Laubach, *Letters by Modern Mystic*, 60.

5. Laubach, *Letters by Modern Mystic*, 61.

6. See discussion of his book *The People of the Philippines* in Dana L. Robert, "The First Globalization: The Internationalization of the Protestant Missionary Movement between the World Wars," *International Bulletin of Missionary Research* 26, no. 2 (April 1, 2002): 50–66.

7. Frank C. Laubach, *Thirty Years with the Silent Billion: Adventuring in Literary* (New York: Fleming H. Revell, 1960), 26.

8. Laubach, *Thirty Years*, 27.

9. February 16, 1930, quoted in Laubach, *Thirty Years*, 30.

10. "Radio Message Given by Dr. Frank Laubach," Frank Laubach Papers, Burke Library Archives, Union Theological Seminary, Columbia University, New York. The following two paragraphs are found in Robert, "Cross-Cultural Friendship," 104.

11. "Radio Message," Laubach Papers.

12. Frank Laubach, in a letter to his father, May 14, 1930, quoted in Laubach, *Thirty Years*, 31.

13. Laubach, *Thirty Years*, 31.

14. Laubach, *Thirty Years*, 33.

15. Quoted in Laubach, *Thirty Years*, 32.

16. Laubach, *Thirty Years*, 32.

17. Peter G. Gowing, "The Legacy of Frank Charles Laubach," *International Bulletin of Missionary Research* 7, no. 2 (April 1, 1983): 58.

18. Laubach, *Thirty Years*, 38.

19. Laubach, *Thirty Years*, 38.

20. Henri J. M. Nouwen, *Adam: God's Beloved* (Maryknoll, NY: Orbis Books, 2012), 16.

21. Henri J. M. Nouwen, *The Return of the Prodigal Son: A Story of Homecoming* (New York: Doubleday, 1994).

22. Jean Vanier, http://www.jean-vanier.org/en/the_man/biography /short_biography.

23. Jean Vanier, *The Gospel of John, the Gospel of Relationship* (Cincinnati: Franciscan Media, 2015) Kindle ed., loc. 62.

24. Nouwen, *Adam*, 47.

25. Nouwen, *Adam*, 48.

26. Nouwen, *Adam*, 48–49.

27. Nouwen, *Adam*, 59.

28. Nouwen, *Adam*, 80.

29. Nouwen, *Adam*, 120.

30. Nouwen, *Adam*, 124.

31. On classical virtues and friendship, see Bennet Helm, "Friendship," Stanford Encyclopedia of Philosophy, https://plato.stanford.edu/entries /friendship/.

32. Evelyne A. Reisacher, *Joyful Witness in the Muslim World: Sharing the Gospel in Everyday Encounters* (Grand Rapids: Baker Academic, 2016), 29.

33. Reisacher, *Joyful Witness*, 40.

34. Reisacher, *Joyful Witness*, 124.

35. Quoted in Reisacher, *Joyful Witness*, 156.

36. Reisacher, *Joyful Witness*, 168.

CHAPTER 7

1. Rudy Rasmus and Kirbyjon Caldwell, *Touch: Pressing against the Wounds of a Broken World* (Nasshville: Thomas Nelson, 2008), 197.

2. Rasmus and Caldwell, *Touch*, 150–51. See also https://www.stjohns downtown.org/meet-the-pastors/.

3. Robert Schreiter, "Reconciliation as a Model of Mission," in *Landmark Essays in Mission and World Christianity*, ed. Robert L. Gallagher and Paul Hertig (Maryknoll, NY: Orbis Books, 2009), 63–72. See also Robert J. Schreiter, *Ministry of Reconciliation: Spirituality and Strategies* (Maryknoll, NY: Orbis Books, 2015).

4. For a classic rejection of the North American "gospel" of efficiency, see Kosuke Koyama, *No Handle on the Cross: An Asian Meditation on the Crucified Mind* (Eugene, OR: Wipf & Stock, 2011).

5. James A. Scherer, *Missionary, Go Home! A Reappraisal of the Christian World Mission* (Englewood Cliffs, NJ: Prentice-Hall, 1964).

6. Dana L. Robert, "Shifting Southward: Global Christianity since 1945," *International Bulletin of Missionary Research* 24, no. 2 (April 1, 2000): 50–58.

7. See the Cultural Competence Inventory at https://idiinventory.com/. David A. Livermore and Chap Clark, *Cultural Intelligence: Improving Your CQ to Engage Our Multicultural World* (Grand Rapids: Baker Academic, 2009).

8. See the classic study of cultural identification in William D. Reyburn, "Identification in the Missionary Task," *Practical Anthropology* 7, no. 1 (1960): 1–15.

9. Leela Gandhi has also argued that (unromantic) same-sex relationships provided a counterwitness to early twentieth-century colonialism and therefore were exceptions to patterns of subordination between cross-cultural partners. Leela Gandhi, *Affective Communities: Anticolonial Thought, Fin-de-Siècle Radicalism, and the Politics of Friendship* (Durham, NC: Duke University Press, 2006). LGBTQ identities add another important but little-researched dimension to cross-cultural friendships among Christians.

10. Personal communication of Dana Robert with Miriam Adeney. See Miriam Adeney, *Kingdom without Borders: The Untold Story of Global Christianity* (Downers Grove, IL: InterVarsity Press, 2009), 270–74.

11. James Gordon Meek et al., "Kayla Mueller in Captivity: Courage, Selflessness as She Defended Christian Faith to ISIS Executioner 'Jihadi John,'" ABC News, August 25, 2016, http://abcnews.go.com/International/kayla-muel ler-captivity-courage-selflessness-defended-christian-faith/story?id=41626763.

12. *Accidental Courtesy: Daryl Davis, Race, and America*, directed by Matt Ornstein (Los Angeles: Sound & Vision, 2017).

13. Quoted in *Accidental Courtesy*.

14. Quoted in *Accidental Courtesy*.

15. Quoted in *Accidental Courtesy*. Note another similar story: "How a Black Man Helped a KKK Leader Leave the Klan," CBN News, August 16, 2017, http://www1.cbn.com/cbnnews/us/2017/may/how-a-black-man-helped -a-kkk-leader-leave-the-klan.

16. As this book is primarily concerned with constructing Christian community, I have not explored the important and related topic of friendship and interfaith dialogue. But openings to the subject can be seen in the case of Merrell Vories's partial embrace of Japanese Shinto in chapter 4, and Frank Laubach's appreciation for Islam in chapter 6.

APPENDIX

1. Gayatri Chakravorty Spivak, *Can the Subaltern Speak?* (Basingstoke, Hampshire: Macmillan, 1988).

INDEX OF NAMES AND SUBJECTS

INDEX OF SCRIPTURE